DREAM THEORY

This book is a work of fiction, created to mimic the appearance of a book that might be seen in a movie or television show. The text within is not meant to be taken seriously. Any resemblance to real-world concepts or ideas is purely coincidental. Please do not attempt to use any of the "techniques" or "concepts" described within this book in real life.

PART 1: THE FOUNDATION OF HYPER-MEMORY

AWAKENING TO HYPER-MEMORY

For centuries, dreams have danced on the fringes of human understanding. Whispered about in myth and folklore, dismissed as mere neurological noise by science, and cherished as intimate portals to the subconscious by artists and poets. But what if dreams held a deeper secret, a key to unlocking a vast reservoir of human experience far beyond our conscious recall? What if dreams weren't just random firings of neurons, but rather, a sophisticated playback system for our minds, replaying the intricate tapestry of our daily lives in breathtaking detail?

This book proposes a radical new theory: **Hyper-Memory**.

Traditional models of memory paint a picture of a fragile archive, selectively storing only the most salient details of our experiences. We remember the highlights, the emotionally charged moments, the facts we deem important. But what about the countless other sensory experiences, the subtle nuances, the fleeting impressions that fade into the background of our conscious awareness? What if these were not lost, but rather, meticulously recorded, waiting to be accessed in the fertile landscape of our dreams?

Imagine this: you walk down a bustling city street, bombarded by a symphony of sights, sounds, and smells. You register faces, conversations snippets, the texture of cobblestones beneath your feet. But in the rush of daily life, these details fade, buried beneath layers of conscious thought and action. Now, imagine entering a dream, not as a passive observer, but as an active participant revisiting that exact street, not as a hazy memory, but in vivid, almost tangible detail. You hear the barista calling out an order, the faint melody from a street musician's guitar, feel the dampness of cobblestones under your shoes – not just remembered, but relived.

This, according to Hyper-Memory theory, is the true potential of dreams. They are not random, nonsensical firings of neurons, but rather, highly detailed ""playback"" sessions, accessing and replaying the vast, unprocessed data of our waking lives.

This book will explore the evidence for this theory, delve into the science of memory and consciousness, and examine how this newfound understanding of dreams can unlock hidden knowledge, forgotten skills, and even unresolved emotional baggage.

Prepare to awaken to a new way of seeing dreams, not just as fleeting glimpses into the subconscious, but as potent portals to a richer, more comprehensive understanding of ourselves and our world. The journey begins here, with Hyper-

Memory.

Through the Looking Glass of Time

Dreams, those enigmatic nocturnal voyages, have captivated humanity since the dawn of consciousness. From ancient cave paintings depicting dream encounters with spirits, to the intricate dream journals kept by philosophers and artists, our fascination with the subconscious realm has woven itself into the fabric of human culture. Yet, our understanding of dreams has shifted dramatically over time, reflecting evolving societal beliefs, scientific advancements, and the enduring human quest to decipher the mysteries of the mind.

Ancient Echoes: Dreams as Divine Whispers

In ancient civilizations, dreams weren't simply fleeting phantoms of the night. They were revered as potent messages from the divine, sacred encounters with ancestors, or even prophetic pronouncements. Egyptians believed dreams were divine revelations, recorded in elaborate dream books alongside hieroglyphics. Mesopotamian priests meticulously interpreted dream symbols, offering guidance on matters of love, war, and even agricultural prosperity.

Across the Aegean Sea, the ancient Greeks saw dreams as conduits to the underworld and the realm of the gods. The oracle at Delphi, famous for its prophetic pronouncements, attributed its visions to the intervention of Apollo, whose priestesses interpreted dreams as messages from the divine. Homer's epic poems, the Iliad and the Odyssey, are rife with dream sequences, often serving as crucial turning points in the narratives, guided by divine intervention or foreshadowing future events.

Even in indigenous cultures worldwide, dreams held profound spiritual significance. Native American tribes saw dreams as portals to the spirit world, offering guidance from animal totems and ancestors. Shamans in Siberian cultures journeyed through dream landscapes, seeking wisdom and healing for themselves and their communities.

The Enlightenment's Rise: Dreams as Physiology, Not Prophecy

The Age of Reason ushered in a shift in perspective. Science began to challenge supernatural explanations, seeking to understand dreams through empirical observation and rational analysis. Thinkers like René Descartes viewed dreams as mere mechanical byproducts of bodily processes, lacking any real meaning.

This trend continued with the emergence of psychoanalysis in the 19th century. Sigmund Freud, the father of psychoanalysis, proposed that dreams were a disguised expression of repressed desires and unconscious conflicts. He emphasized the symbolic language of dreams, suggesting that interpreting these symbols could unlock hidden psychological truths.

While Freud's theories sparked debate and revolutionized our understanding of the unconscious mind, they ultimately positioned dreams as products of the brain, rather than windows to a spiritual realm.

Modern Neuroscience: Bridging the Gap

Today, neuroscience stands at a fascinating

crossroads, bridging the gap between the ancient fascination with dreams and the scientific quest for understanding. Advancements in neuroimaging have allowed researchers to observe brain activity during dreaming, revealing complex patterns of neural firing that mirror waking memory processes.

While we still grapple with the precise nature of dream content and its relationship to waking consciousness, emerging research suggests that dreams might not be simply random firings of neurons, but rather, intricate replays of our experiences, potentially serving a crucial role in memory consolidation, emotional processing, and even creative insight.

From Mysticism to Mechanism: A Continuum of Understanding

The journey of understanding dreams has taken us from ancient reverence to scientific inquiry, from mystical interpretations to neurological investigations. While our grasp of the dream world remains incomplete, the shift from viewing dreams as mere fleeting phantoms to recognizing their potential as rich sources of information and insights has been profound.

As we delve deeper into the realm of Hyper-Memory, we stand poised to build upon this evolving understanding, exploring how dreams might hold not just glimpses into the subconscious, but a vast, untapped reservoir of our lived experiences, waiting to be accessed and decoded.

The Memory Maze: When Traditional Models Fall Short

For decades, the dominant model of memory has been akin to a filing cabinet: information is stored in discrete "files," consciously encoded and retrieved when needed. However, this tidy metaphor falls short when confronted with the complexities of human experience. Traditional memory models struggle to account for several intriguing phenomena that suggest a deeper, more multifaceted reality to how we store and access information – phenomena that Hyper-Memory seeks to explain.

1. The "Tip-of-the-Tongue" Enigma:

The tip-of-the-tongue phenomenon - a frustratingly familiar experience indeed. It's as if the information we seek is hiding just beyond our grasp, teasing us with its proximity yet remaining elusive. This common occurrence challenges our traditional understanding of memory as neatly organized files, waiting to be retrieved. But what if these "forgotten" fragments aren't lost at all? What if they reside in the dream realm, waiting to be accessed through a different kind of retrieval mechanism - a playback rather than a search?

Hyper-Memory proposes that our dreams hold the key to unlocking these hidden memories. By tapping into our subconscious mind, we may be able to retrieve information that lies beyond the reach of our conscious memory. This playback mechanism could allow us to access memories that are currently inaccessible, providing a new window into our past experiences and knowledge.

But how do we tap into this dream realm? How do we access these hidden memories and bring them into our conscious awareness? Hyper-Memory suggests that the answer lies in the practice of lucid dreaming - the ability to consciously navigate our dreams and access the subconscious mind. By becoming aware of our dreams and taking control of our subconscious thoughts, we may be able to unlock the secrets of our hidden memories and tap into the vast reservoir of knowledge that lies within us.

Furthermore, Hyper-Memory proposes that our dreams are not just random firings of our brain, but rather a complex language that our subconscious mind uses to communicate with us. By learning to decipher this language, we may be able to tap into the hidden memories that lie within our dreams and unlock the secrets of our subconscious mind.

2. Flashbulb Memories: Faded Details, Vivid Emotion

Flashbulb memories - those vivid, emotionally charged recollections that feel startlingly detailed. They're like snapshots in time, capturing the essence of a historical event or personal tragedy with striking clarity. Yet, despite their intensity, these memories are often prone to distortion over time. Minor details change or become embellished, like a game of telephone where the original message becomes altered with each retelling. Traditional models suggest that emotionally significant events are encoded more strongly in our memory, but why this distortion? Why do these vivid memories become susceptible to change over time?

Hyper-Memory proposes that flashbulb memories might not be perfectly stored files, but rather, replayed "recordings" that become susceptible to emotional bias and subsequent reinterpretation during retelling. This means that each time we recall a flashbulb memory, we're not accessing a static file, but rather, replaying a dynamic recording that can be influenced by our emotions and experiences. This replaying process can lead to subtle changes in the memory over time, as our emotions and biases shape the way we recall the event.

Furthermore, Hyper-Memory suggests that the act of retelling flashbulb memories can itself become a form of emotional reinterpretation. Each time we share a vivid memory with others, we're not only replaying the recording but also reframing it through our current emotional lens. This reframing process can lead to further distortions in the memory, as our emotions and biases shape the way we recall and retell the event.

The implications of Hyper-Memory's theory on flashbulb memories are far-reaching. If our vivid memories are not fixed files but rather dynamic recordings, then our understanding of memory itself must be revised. This challenges the traditional view of memory as a passive storage system, where information is simply recorded and retrieved. Instead, Hyper-Memory suggests that memory is an active process, where information is constantly being replayed, reinterpreted, and revised.

This dynamic view of memory also raises questions about the accuracy of eyewitness testimony. If flashbulb memories are prone to distortion over time, then how reliable are they as evidence in criminal trials? Hyper-Memory's theory suggests that eyewitness testimony should be treated with caution, as it may be influenced by emotional bias and subsequent reinterpretation. This challenges the traditional reliance on eyewitness testimony as a cornerstone of forensic evidence.

Furthermore, Hyper-Memory's theory has implications for our understanding of historical events. If flashbulb memories are prone to distortion over time, then how accurate are our historical records? Hyper-Memory suggests that historical events may be subject to reinterpretation over time, as subsequent generations reframe the past through their own emotional biases. This challenges the traditional view of history as a fixed narrative, instead suggesting that history is a dynamic and evolving story.

3. The Fragmented Nature of Experience:

Consider a bustling city street scene: the sights, sounds, and sensations that bombard our senses. We register faces, snippets of conversations, the texture of cobblestones beneath our feet. But can we truly recall every single detail with perfect clarity? Traditional models struggle to account for this inherent fragmentation of experience. Our memories are like puzzle pieces, scattered and disjointed, rather than a seamless narrative.

Hyper-Memory posits that dreams might act as a "playback" system that reconstructs these fragmented sensory experiences, stitching together a more holistic, albeit potentially dream-like, tapestry of the original event. During sleep, our brains replay and process the day's experiences, weaving together the disparate threads of memory into a more cohesive narrative. This playback mechanism allows us to relive and reinterpret our experiences, filling in gaps and consolidating memories.

But how does this playback system work? Hyper-Memory suggests that the brain uses a combination of sensory and emotional cues to reconstruct the original event. By replaying the sights, sounds, and sensations associated with a particular memory, the brain can reconstitute the experience and fill in any gaps. This process is thought to occur during the REM stage of sleep, when the brain is most active and dreams are most vivid. Furthermore, Hyper-Memory proposes that this playback system can also influence our emotional responses to memories. By replaying and reinterpreting our experiences, we can reframe our emotional associations with particular memories. This can lead to a process of emotional consolidation, where we integrate new emotional insights into our existing memories. This process can help us better understand ourselves and our place in the world.

4. The Unconscious Architect of Memory:

Our conscious mind actively filters and interprets information, shaping our memories based on pre-existing beliefs and biases. This process of conscious encoding and retrieval is well understood, but what about the vast amount of information processed subconsciously? The subtle nuances, fleeting impressions, and emotional undercurrents that escape conscious awareness are often overlooked, yet they hold significant value in understanding our thoughts, feelings, and behaviors.

Hyper-Memory suggests that dreams might serve as a platform for accessing this subconscious "archive," replaying experiences in their raw, unfiltered form. During sleep, our brains process and consolidate information from the day, including the subconscious thoughts and feelings that we may not have been aware of. This processing can lead to the creation of dreams that reflect our subconscious mind, providing a window into our deepest thoughts and desires.

But how do we access this subconscious archive? Hyper-Memory proposes that the key lies in the practice of lucid dreaming - the ability to consciously navigate and control our dreams. By becoming aware of our dreams and taking control of our subconscious mind, we may be able to unlock the secrets of our subconscious archive and gain insight into our deepest thoughts and desires.

Furthermore, Hyper-Memory suggests that the subconscious archive is not just a passive repository of information, but an active participant in shaping our thoughts and behaviors. By accessing and interpreting the contents of our subconscious archive, we may be able to gain a deeper understanding of ourselves and the world around us. This can lead to greater self-awareness, improved decision-making, and enhanced creativity.

The Hyper-Memory theory posits that the subconscious mind plays a crucial role in the processing and consolidation of memories, particularly during the REM stage of sleep. This stage is characterized by heightened brain activity, vivid dreams, and the replaying of neural patterns associated with previously experienced events.

During REM sleep, the brain's neurotransmitters, such as norepinephrine, serotonin, and acetylcholine, are deactivated, allowing for the unregulated flow of information between different brain regions. This neural activity is thought to facilitate the consolidation of memories from the hippocampus to the neocortex, where they can be stored for long-term retrieval.

The Hyper-Memory theory suggests that the subconscious mind acts as a "black box" that processes and interprets the vast amount of sensory information we receive throughout the day. This information is then consolidated into memories during REM sleep, where it can be replayed and refined through the process of neural plasticity. By accessing the subconscious mind through techniques such as lucid dreaming or meditation, individuals may be able to tap into this vast reservoir of information and gain insight into their thoughts, feelings, and behaviors. This can lead to greater self-awareness, improved decision-making, and enhanced creativity.

5. The Case for Beyond-Logical Access:

Dreams often defy logic and linear narrative, weaving together seemingly disparate elements, defying temporal constraints, and accessing information in ways that seem illogical during waking hours. This "dream logic" might suggest that dreams operate on a different set of rules, potentially allowing us to access information stored in ways beyond our conscious comprehension.

These limitations of traditional memory models highlight the need for a more expansive framework, one that embraces the multifaceted nature of human experience and acknowledges the potential of dreams as powerful tools for accessing, replaying, and ultimately, understanding the vast tapestry of our lives. Hyper-Memory offers a compelling alternative, suggesting that dreams are not mere remnants of the night, but gateways to a rich, untapped realm of memory waiting to be explored.

Whispers from the Dreaming Brain:
Scientific Clues & Emerging Research

While the concept of dreams as detailed memory replays might sound fantastical, emerging research in neuroscience and psychology offers intriguing clues supporting this possibility. It's not conclusive proof, but a growing body of evidence hinting at a deeper connection between dreams and memory than previously thought.

Here are some key areas where science is shedding light on the potential for dream-based memory retrieval:

1. Neuroimaging Reveals Dream-Recall Patterns:

Functional Magnetic Resonance Imaging (fMRI) studies have revealed fascinating patterns of brain activity during dreaming. Researchers have observed activation in regions associated with memory processing, including the hippocampus and the prefrontal cortex. These regions are crucial for memory consolidation and retrieval, and their activation during dreaming suggests that dreams might not be just random neural firings, but rather, involve processes similar to accessing and reactivating stored memories.

The hippocampus, in particular, is thought to play a key role in memory consolidation, helping to transfer information from short-term to long-term memory. During dreaming, the hippocampus is active, suggesting that dreams might be involved in the consolidation of memories, especially emotional ones. This is consistent with the idea that dreams help us process and make sense of our experiences, especially those that are emotionally charged. The prefrontal cortex, on the other hand, is involved in retrieving and manipulating information stored in memory. During dreaming, the prefrontal cortex is also active, suggesting that dreams might be involved in the retrieval and reconstruction of memories. This is consistent with the idea that dreams help us make sense of our experiences by replaying and reinterpreting them in different ways.

Furthermore, the activation of these regions during dreaming suggests that dreams might be involved in the formation of new memories, especially those that are emotionally charged. This is consistent with the idea that dreams help us process and make sense of our experiences, especially those that are emotionally charged. By replaying and reinterpreting these experiences in different ways, dreams might help us form new memories that are more vivid and emotionally charged.

2. Lucid Dreaming: Conscious Access to Dream Content:

The ability to become aware within a dream, known as lucid dreaming, offers a unique window into dream content. Lucid dreamers can often recall details with remarkable clarity upon waking, suggesting that the brain possesses mechanisms for accessing and manipulating dream "memories" in a conscious manner. While not everyone experiences lucid dreaming, its existence challenges the notion that dreams are purely unconscious phenomena and suggests a potential for conscious interaction with dream-based information.

3. The Déjà Vu Phenomenon: Glimpses of Dream Replay?

That eerie feeling of déjà vu, of having experienced something before despite knowing you haven't, might hold a clue to the mysteries of our minds. Some researchers propose that déjà vu could be triggered by involuntary "playback" snippets from dreams, where a waking experience briefly aligns with a dream scenario, creating a sense of familiarity. This idea suggests that our dreams might be more closely tied to our waking reality than we previously thought, and that the line between the two might be more blurred than we realize.

Imagine walking down a familiar street, and suddenly feeling like you've already experienced this moment before. The buildings, the people, the sounds - everything feels eerily familiar, despite knowing you've never been here before. This is déjà vu, a feeling that's both fascinating and unsettling. And according to some researchers, it might be triggered by our dreams.

The idea is that our dreams can influence our waking experiences, creating a sense of familiarity or déjà vu. This could happen when a waking experience aligns with a dream scenario, triggering a feeling of recognition or familiarity. It's as if our brain is saying, "Hey, I've seen this before - in my dreams!"

While this idea is still speculative, it highlights the complex and mysterious nature of our minds. Our dreams and waking experiences are intertwined in ways we're still discovering, and the line between reality and fantasy is often blurred. By exploring the mysteries of déjà vu and dreams, we might uncover new insights into the workings of our minds and the nature of reality itself.

4. Sleep and Memory Consolidation:

Research has long established the crucial role of sleep, particularly slow-wave sleep, in memory consolidation. During this phase, the hippocampus replays and strengthens memories from the previous day, transferring them to long-term storage. This process is essential for learning and memory, as it allows us to retain information and skills over time. It's conceivable that dreams, occurring predominantly during REM sleep, might play a role in this "replay" process, contributing to a more thorough and detailed consolidation of experiences. During REM sleep, the brain is active and dreams are more vivid and intense. This increased activity could be related to the processing and consolidation of memories, especially emotional ones.

Research has shown that the brain regions

involved in emotion, such as the amygdala, are active during REM sleep and dreaming. This suggests that dreams might be involved in the processing and consolidation of emotional memories, which are typically more vivid and memorable than neutral ones.

Furthermore, the replay process during REM sleep might not only be limited to emotional memories but also to other types of experiences. For example, research has shown that the brain replays and consolidates motor skills during REM sleep, which can improve performance in tasks that require motor coordination.

Overall, the relationship between dreams and memory consolidation is complex and not yet fully understood. However, research suggests that dreams might play a role in the replay and consolidation of experiences, especially emotional ones, during REM sleep.

5. Animal Studies: Echoes Across Species:

Studies on animals, particularly rodents, have shown fascinating parallels between dream behavior and memory processes. Rats, for instance, exhibit REM sleep-like activity patterns and display altered responses to environmental stimuli after dreaming, suggesting that dream-related memory replay might be a conserved biological function across species.

Research on rodents has revealed that they exhibit similar brain wave patterns during REM sleep as humans, characterized by rapid eye movements, increased neural activity, and vivid dreams. These dreams are thought to be involved in the consolidation of memories, particularly those related to spatial navigation and emotional experiences.

One study found that rats who were trained to navigate a maze and then deprived of REM sleep performed poorly on subsequent maze trials, suggesting that REM sleep and dreaming are essential for memory consolidation. Another study found that rats who were exposed to a stressful event and then allowed to enter REM sleep showed reduced stress responses and improved memory consolidation, suggesting that dreaming may help to process and integrate emotional experiences.

These findings suggest that the function of dreams in memory consolidation may be conserved across species, and that studying dream behavior in animals may provide insights into the neural mechanisms underlying human dreaming and memory. By exploring the parallels between dream behavior and memory processes in animals, we may gain a deeper understanding of the complex and mysterious nature of our own dreams and memories.

Looking Ahead: Unraveling the Dream Code:

While these scientific clues are intriguing, it's crucial to emphasize that research on dream-based memory is still in its early stages. We need further investigation to definitively establish the mechanisms at play and the precise extent to which dreams function as a playback system for our experiences.

Nevertheless, the converging evidence paints a compelling picture: dreams might not merely be fleeting nocturnal phantoms but rather, active participants in the intricate tapestry of human memory, offering a unique and potentially powerful pathway for accessing and understanding the rich complexities of our lived experiences.

The "Hyper-Memory" theory invites us to reimagine the nature of dreams, venturing beyond traditional interpretations to unlock a deeper understanding of the sleeping mind and its profound potential.

SENSORY SYMPHONY OF DREAMS

Imagine this: you're walking through a bustling marketplace in a dream. It's not just the vibrant colors of silk fabrics and overflowing fruit stalls that register, but also the symphony of sounds swirling around you – the boisterous haggling of vendors, the rhythmic clang of a blacksmith's hammer, the lilting melody of a distant lute. You catch the scent of spiced pastries wafting from a nearby stall, feel the rough texture of woven baskets beneath your fingertips, and even experience the subtle, prickly sensation of a sunbeam warming your face.

This isn't just a vivid visual experience; it's a multi-sensory replay, a ""playback"" of your senses captured with remarkable fidelity. Hyper-Memory theory proposes that dreams aren't merely visual narratives, but rather, immersive reconstructions that encompass a full spectrum of sensory experiences, replaying not only what we saw, but also what we heard, smelled, tasted, touched, and felt emotionally.

Opening the Senses: Beyond the Visual Canvas

For generations, we've viewed dreams primarily as visual spectacles – fleeting images flickering across the mental screen. We remember the vivid landscapes, the fantastical creatures, the fleeting faces, but what about the symphony of experiences that accompanies these visuals?

Think back to a vivid dream. Was it simply a parade of pictures? Or did you hear whispers, feel textures, even smell the air thick with the scent of rain or freshly baked bread?

Hyper-Memory theory proposes that dreams are not merely visual narratives, but rather, immersive reconstructions that encompass a full spectrum of sensory experience. Imagine them not as silent movies, but as multi-sensory symphonies, where sights, sounds, smells, textures, and emotions intertwine to create a holistic replay of lived experiences.

It's not just about seeing the bustling marketplace; it's about hearing the vendors' cries, feeling the cobblestones beneath your feet, smelling the spices wafting from a nearby stall. It's about tasting the sweetness of ripe fruit and feeling the warmth of the sun on your skin. These sensory details, often overlooked in traditional memory models, become crucial pieces of the dream puzzle, enriching the playback and potentially unlocking a deeper level of recall.

This sensory richness challenges the idea that dreams are simply random neural firings. It suggests that our brains meticulously record not just visual information, but a full orchestra of sensory data, waiting to be revisited in vivid detail within the dream realm.

Beyond Sight: The Symphony of Other Senses

While dreams are often remembered as visual spectacles, Hyper-Memory theory proposes they encompass a far richer sensory tapestry.

Imagine not just seeing a childhood memory, but truly *reliving* it through a symphony of senses beyond sight:

1. Auditory Echoes: The Soundtrack of Memory

Sound plays a profound role in shaping our memories. A particular melody, a loved one's voice, the clatter of rain on a rooftop – these auditory cues can instantly transport us back in time. Dreams, according to this theory, tap into this sonic archive, allowing us to hear not just ambient noise, but specific sounds that were present during the original experience.

Think about it:

Reliving a childhood concert: Not just

seeing the stage, but hearing the roar of the crowd, the thrumming of the bass, and the soaring notes of your favorite song. The memories come flooding back, transporting you to a time when life was simpler, and the music was everything. You remember the excitement of arriving at the venue, the anticipation building as you waited for the doors to open. The rush of adrenaline as you took your place in the crowd, surrounded by fellow fans all sharing in the same excitement. The lights dimmed, and the band took the stage, launching into the opening chords of their first song. The crowd erupted into cheers, and you were swept up in the energy of the moment. The music was loud, the bass thumping through your chest, and the melodies soaring above the din. You sang along to every word, lost in the music and the moment. The band played all their hits, and you danced and sang along to each one. The concert was a blur of color and sound, a kaleidoscope of emotions and experiences. And now, years later, you can still remember the thrill of that concert, the music and the moment etched into your memory like a scar. You can still hear the roar of the crowd, the thrumming of the bass, and the soaring notes of your favorite song. The memory is vivid, alive, and still resonating deep within your soul.

Recalling a poignant conversation: Hearing your deceased grandmother's voice again, whispering words of wisdom, even though she's no longer physically present. The memory is vivid, as if she's sitting right next to you, her warm breath on your ear, her gentle tone soothing your soul. You remember the conversation like it was yesterday, the way she listened attentively to your concerns, the way she offered words of wisdom and comfort. Her voice was like a balm to your soul, calming your fears and soothing your doubts. As you recall the conversation, you can almost hear her voice again, whispering words of encouragement and support. It's as if she's still with you, guiding you through life's challenges and celebrating its triumphs. The memory is so vivid that you can almost smell the scent of her perfume, feel the warmth of her embrace, and taste the sweetness of her cooking. It's as if she's still with you, in every way that matters. This is the power of memory, the ability to recall and relive moments from our past, to bring back to life the people and experiences that have shaped us into who we are today. It's a gift, a treasure that we should cherish and honor, and use to guide us on our journey through life.

Experiencing the bustling energy of a city street: Hearing the rumble of buses, the chatter of pedestrians, the distant wail of a siren – a full soundscape that immerses you back into that urban environment. The sounds are so vivid, so real, that you can almost smell the exhaust fumes, feel the rush of the wind, and taste the street food. The rumble of buses is like thunder in the distance, growing louder as they approach. The chatter of pedestrians is a constant hum, a never-ending stream of conversation and laughter. The wail of sirens is a piercing cry, cutting through the din and demanding attention. As you stand on the sidewalk, the sounds swirl around you, a kaleidoscope of noise and color. The city is alive, pulsing with energy and vitality. You feel the rhythm of the streets, the beat of the city's heart. The soundscape is so immersive that you can almost see the city around you, the towering skyscrapers, the bustling streets, the vibrant markets. You can almost taste the food, the street vendors selling their wares, the restaurants serving up culinary delights. The city is a sensory feast, a never-ending buffet of sights, sounds, and smells. And as you stand on the sidewalk, taking it all in, you feel alive, connected to the pulsing heart of the city.

2. Olfactory Immersion: Scents as Memory Keys

Smell is often linked to the most potent and evocative memories. A whiff of freshly baked bread can conjure up childhood memories, while a particular perfume might transport you back to a first date. Dreams might tap into this powerful olfactory connection, allowing you to not just see a place, but to *smell* it with startling clarity.

Imagine:

Returning to your childhood home: Not just picturing its layout, but smelling the aroma of your mother's apple pie baking in the oven.

The memory is so vivid, so real, that you can almost taste the sweetness of the apples, the flakiness of the crust, and the warmth of the love that went into making it. You remember walking into the kitchen, the aroma of cinnamon and sugar filling your nostrils, making your mouth water in anticipation. Your mother, busy at the counter, would smile and say, "Almost ready, dear!" And you would wait patiently, watching as she carefully placed the pie in the oven, the timer ticking away until it was perfectly golden brown. The smell of apple pie is more than just a scent; it's a memory trigger, transporting you back to a time when life was simpler, when love and warmth filled your home. It's a reminder of the joy and comfort that food can bring, the way it can evoke emotions and create memories that last a lifetime. As you sit here, remembering the smell of your mother's apple pie, you can almost feel the warmth of her love, the comfort of her presence. It's as if she's still with you, baking in the kitchen, filling your heart with joy and your senses with the sweet aroma of apple pie.

Stepping into a romantic garden: Recreating not just the visual beauty of blooming flowers, but the intoxicating scent of jasmine and honeysuckle filling the air. The memory is so vivid, so real, that you can almost feel the soft petals of the flowers, the gentle rustle of the leaves, and the warm sun on your skin. As you walk through the garden, the scent of jasmine and honeysuckle envelops you, transporting you to a place of serenity and peace. The air is filled with the sweet aroma of blooming flowers, and the gentle hum of bees as they flit from flower to flower. The visual beauty of the garden is breathtaking, with vibrant colors and delicate petals. The flowers sway gently in the breeze, creating a sense of movement and life. The garden is a place of beauty, a place of peace, and a place of tranquility. As you walk through the garden, you feel a sense of connection to nature, a sense of connection to the beauty and wonder of the world around you. The garden is a place of solace, a place of refuge, and a place of peace. It is a place where you can escape the stresses and worries of everyday life, and connect with the beauty and wonder of the world around you.

Reliving a camping trip: Smelling the campfire smoke, the damp earth, and the pine needles underfoot, transporting you back to that rustic wilderness. The memories come flooding back, and you can almost hear the crackling of the fire, the chirping of the crickets, and the rustling of leaves in the wind. You remember setting up camp, the smell of damp earth and pine needles filling your nostrils as you pitched your tent. The sound of the campfire crackling, the warmth of the flames on your skin, and the smell of sizzling marshmallows and hot dogs wafting through the air. As you sit around the campfire, roasting marshmallows and swapping stories, the stars twinkle above, and the sound of the wind rustling through the trees creates a sense of peace and tranquility. The campfire smoke fills your lungs, and the smell of pine needles and damp earth transports you to a place of serenity and connection with nature. The memories of that camping trip are etched in your mind, a reminder of the beauty and wonder of the great outdoors. The smell of campfire smoke, the sound of rustling leaves, and the feel of pine needles underfoot are all triggers that transport you back to that place of peace and tranquility.

3. Tactile Replay: Feeling the World Again

Touch is another vital sense often overlooked in traditional dream narratives. Hyper-Memory suggests dreams can recreate not just visual images, but also the textures and physical sensations associated with those experiences.

Think about:

Holding a loved one's hand: Feeling the warmth of their skin, the gentle pressure of their fingers, a tactile connection that transcends distance. The memory is so vivid, so real, that you can almost feel the beat of their heart, the rhythm of their breath, and the comfort of their presence. You remember the way their hand felt in yours, the way their fingers intertwined with yours, creating a sense of unity and connection. The warmth of their skin radiated into yours, creating a sense of comfort and security. The gentle pressure of their fingers was a reminder of their love and support, a reminder that they were always there for you. As you hold their hand in your memory, you feel a sense of peace and tranquility wash over you. The world around you melts away, and all that's left is the two of you, connected in a way that transcends words and distance. The love and connection you feel is palpable, a reminder of the bond you share. The memory of holding their hand is a reminder of the power of touch, the power of love, and the power of connection. It's a reminder that even in the darkest of times, there is always hope, always love, and always a way to connect with those who matter most.

Walking barefoot on sand: Not just seeing the beach, but feeling the coolness of the sand between your toes, the sun-warmed grains beneath your feet. The sensation is so vivid, so real, that you can almost feel the sand shifting beneath your weight, the gentle slope of the dune, and the ocean breeze rustling your hair. You remember the feeling of the sand between your toes, the way it shifted and slid as you walked. The coolness of the sand was a welcome relief from the warmth of the sun, and the sensation of the grains slipping away from your feet was like a gentle massage. The sound of the waves crashing in the distance added to the sense of relaxation, and the smell of saltwater and seaweed filled your nostrils. As you walk along the beach, the sand feels cool and soft beneath your feet. You can feel the texture of the grains, the way they shift and slide as you move. The sensation is calming, soothing, and peaceful. You feel connected to the natural world, to the earth and the sea. The sound of the waves, the smell of the saltwater, and the feel of the sand between your toes all combine to create a sense of tranquility and relaxation.

Crafting with clay: Recreating the smooth, malleable texture of the clay, the coolness of the water used to shape it, a sensory echo of the creative act. The memory is so vivid, so real, that you can almost feel the clay yielding to your touch, the water dripping from your fingers, and the satisfaction of creating something with your own hands. You remember the sensation of the clay between your fingers, the way it responded to your touch, the way it could be molded and shaped into whatever form you desired. The coolness of the water was a refreshing contrast to the warmth of your hands, and the sound of the water dripping was like music to your ears. As you worked with the clay, you felt a sense of connection to the earth, to the natural world. The clay was a part of the earth, and you were shaping it, molding it, creating something new and unique. The process was meditative, calming, and fulfilling. The memory of crafting with clay is a sensory echo of the creative act, a reminder of the joy and satisfaction of creating something with your own hands. It's a reminder of the connection to the natural world, and the power of creativity to shape and mold our lives.

4. Gustatory Glimpses: Tastes as Memory Triggers

While less commonly recalled, dreams can potentially recreate taste experiences as well. Imagine:

Sampling exotic food in a dream market: Not just seeing the vibrant dishes, but savoring their flavors - the tang of spices, the sweetness of mangoes, the richness of chocolate. The memory is so vivid, so real, that you can almost smell the aromas wafting through the air, the sizzle of the food on the grills, and the chatter of the vendors calling out their wares. You remember walking through the market, the sights and sounds overwhelming your senses. The colors of the spices, the fruits, and the vegetables were like a rainbow, each one more vibrant than the last. The smells of the food were intoxicating, the aromas of spices, herbs, and grilled meats filling your nostrils. As you sampled the food, the flavors exploded on your tongue. The tang of the spices, the sweetness of the mangoes, and the richness of the chocolate were like a symphony of flavors. Each bite was a new discovery, a new sensation that left you wanting more. The memory of the dream market is a sensory experience that stays with you, a reminder of the power of food to evoke emotions and create memories. The sights, sounds, and smells of the market are etched in your memory, a vivid reminder of the joy of discovery and the pleasure of the senses.

Returning to your grandmother's kitchen: Not just picturing her baking, but tasting her signature cinnamon rolls, their warm, comforting flavor filling your dream palate. The memory is so vivid, so real, that you can almost smell the sweet aroma of cinnamon and sugar wafting from the oven, the sound of her gentle humming as she works, and the feel of her warm, flour-dusted hands on your face. You remember the way the cinnamon rolls looked, golden brown and fluffy, with a sweet glaze drizzled on top. The way they tasted, warm and comforting, with a hint of cinnamon and sugar. The way they made you feel, like you were home, like you were loved. As you sit in your grandmother's kitchen, surrounded by the sights and smells of her baking, you feel a sense of peace and comfort wash over you. The world outside fades away, and all that's left is the warmth and love of her kitchen. The cinnamon rolls are more than just a treat, they're a symbol of her love and care, a reminder of the happy times you shared together.

5. Emotional Echoes: Feelings Amplified in Dreams

Beyond sensory details, dreams can heighten the emotional resonance of recalled experiences. A seemingly mundane event might surface in a dream, not just visually, but also with the full force of the emotions felt at the time – joy, sadness, anxiety, excitement.

This emotional amplification could provide valuable insights into our past, helping us process unresolved feelings or gain new perspectives on past events.

By weaving together these multi-sensory threads, Hyper-Memory theory proposes that dreams offer a richer, more immersive experience than mere visual recall. They become portals to a deeper level of memory, allowing us to relive not just what we saw, but what we heard, smelled, touched, tasted, and felt – a symphony of sensory experience that enriches our understanding of ourselves and our past.

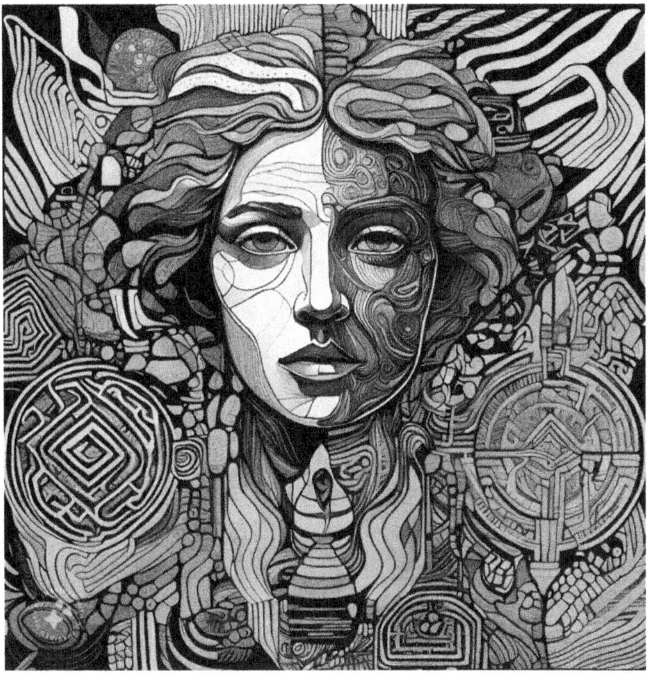

BEYOND VISUAL RECALL

Traditional memory models often focus on consciously retrieving facts and events, but what happens when memories reside not just in conscious files, but in a vast, immersive archive accessible through dreams? Hyper-Memory theory suggests that dreams could act as playback mechanisms, replaying not just visual details, but also forgotten knowledge, skills, and even languages, encoded within the sensory tapestry of our experiences.

Let's explore some compelling examples:

1. The Linguist's Dream Dictionary: Reviving Lost Tongues

Dr. Reed, a retired linguist specializing in ancient Sumerian, dreamt vividly for months about a marketplace scene, filled with bustling activity and conversations in an unfamiliar language. While she couldn't fully decipher it upon waking, she noticed recurring patterns, specific sounds, and even grammatical structures. Intrigued, she started meticulously journaling her dreams, meticulously recording each phrase and sound. After weeks of analysis, she noticed striking similarities between her dream "language" and fragments of ancient Sumerian texts. She consulted with colleagues, and eventually, through a combination of dream-derived insights and academic research, Dr. Reed was able to "decode" her dream language, unearthing new linguistic insights into a lost civilization. This case, while anecdotal, hints at the potential for dreams to unlock dormant knowledge, bridging the gap between forgotten languages and conscious understanding.

2. The Artist's Forgotten Technique: A Dream-Inspired Masterpiece

Michel, a talented painter, suffered a debilitating stroke that impaired his fine motor skills, leaving him unable to paint with his usual dexterity. Months later, while struggling with his easel, he had a vivid dream depicting his younger self effortlessly executing a complex brushstroke technique he hadn't consciously used in years. Upon waking, he struggled to recall the specific motion, but the dream imagery remained vivid. Determined, Michel practiced the movements he envisioned in his dream, slowly regaining the lost technique. He ultimately created a new series of paintings, drawing inspiration and mastery from this dream-recalled skill, demonstrating how dreams can potentially reactivate dormant artistic abilities.

3. The Musician's Melody from the Beyond: A Haunting Encore

Maria, a grieving musician, lost her father suddenly, leaving behind unfinished musical compositions. One night, she dreamt vividly of him, playing a complex melody on his cherished piano. The tune was both familiar and unfamiliar, echoing fragments of his past compositions but also weaving new, hauntingly beautiful notes. Upon waking, Maria struggled to fully recall the melody, but the feeling of its haunting beauty remained. She painstakingly worked to reconstruct the dream melody, recording fragments, jotting down notes, and gradually piecing together her father's unfinished masterpiece. His music, seemingly preserved in the dream realm, became a poignant tribute and a testament to the potential for dreams to preserve and deliver artistic legacies beyond conscious memory.

Beyond Anecdotes: A Glimpse into the Potential

While these stories might be anecdotal, they point to a fascinating possibility – that dreams could act as repositories for knowledge, skills, and creative inspiration, waiting to be accessed through the playback mechanism of Hyper-Memory.

Further research into dream recall and its potential to unlock forgotten expertise, languages, and artistic expression could revolutionize our understanding of memory and its role in human creativity, healing, and personal growth.

PART 2: HARNESSING DREAM RECALL

THE DREAM ARCHITECT

Beyond Passive Sleep: Actively Shaping Dreamscapes

For centuries, we've treated sleep as a passive state – a nightly surrender to unconsciousness, a time to simply ""recharge"" our batteries. But what if we told you that sleep could be more than just an inert state? What if we could actively shape our nocturnal journeys, transforming them from passive drifting into intentional voyages of exploration?

Welcome to the world of the "Dream Architect." This isn't about controlling our dreams, forcing specific narratives, or manipulating dream content like puppeteers pulling strings. It's about consciously crafting our sleep environments to prime our brains for vivid, detailed dream recall – to unlock the vast, intricate landscapes already residing within our subconscious. Think of it as building a bespoke dreamscape, one carefully curated to maximize the playback potential of our nightly adventures.

Imagine:

Instead of waking with vague fragments of forgotten dreams, you consistently recall full-fledged narratives, rich in sensory detail, emotions, and insights.

You access forgotten knowledge, long-lost skills, or creative sparks hidden within the tapestry of your dream experiences, sparking fresh perspectives and breakthroughs.

You journey back to pivotal moments in your life, reliving them not just visually, but with the full sensory richness of the original experience – the scent of your grandmother's baking, the feel of a childhood playground swing, the echo of laughter long silenced.

This might sound like something out of science fiction, but the potential is grounded in emerging research exploring the intricate interplay between sleep, memory, and dream recall.

By understanding how our surroundings, sensory cues, and even our own intentions can influence dream activity, we can become active participants in our own nocturnal journeys, transforming sleep from a passive escape to a conscious exploration of our inner worlds.

Get ready to become a Dream Architect. It's

time to awaken to the extraordinary possibilities within our dreams.

Visual Cues: Painting a Dreamscape with Light and Imagery

Vision plays a dominant role in our waking world, and it holds significant influence within dreams too. To prime the brain for vivid visual recall, "Dream Architects" can strategically manipulate their visual environment. Remember, the goal isn't to bombard the brain with overwhelming visuals, but to subtly guide and enhance natural dream imagery:

1. Embrace Darkness: The Night Sky Advantage:

2. Minimize Light Pollution: Darkness is crucial for melatonin production, a

hormone essential for deep sleep and vivid dreaming.

o Block out street lights with blackout curtains, cover electronic device LEDs, and avoid bright nightlights.

3. Opt for Gradual Dimming: Instead of sudden darkness, use dimmers on bedside lamps or smart lighting systems that gradually lower brightness as bedtime approaches, mimicking natural dusk.

4. Strategic Soft Lighting: Illuminating the Dream Gateways:

o Red Light Sanctuary: Red light has the least disruptive effect on melatonin production. Consider using dim red-spectrum bulbs near the bed or salt lamps for a calming, sleep-promoting glow without harsh brightness.

o Moonlight Mimicry: Moonlight-like lamps that emit a gentle, diffused white light can create a serene ambiance reminiscent of natural moonlight, potentially influencing dream themes toward nature and tranquility.

5. Visual Cues as Dream Seeds: Planting Subliminal Themes:

o Dream-Inspiring Imagery: Posters, artwork, or even projectors displaying nature scenes, abstract patterns, or images related to desired dream themes near the bed can subtly influence the visual fabric of dreams.

- Avoid overly chaotic or jarring imagery – keep it calming and evocative.

6. Beyond Still Images: Moving Visuals with Caution:

- Gentle Projected Patterns: Very subtle, slow-moving patterns (stars, waves, mandalas) projected onto the ceiling might provide gentle visual stimulation, potentially influencing dream content.

- Caution with Videos: While tempting, avoid watching stimulating or emotionally charged videos right before sleep, as they can interfere with restful sleep and potentially lead to disturbing dreams.

Remember: Visual cues are powerful, but they should be subtle and chosen thoughtfully. The goal is to create a conducive atmosphere for your brain to weave its own dream narratives, enriched by these visual prompts.

Further research and experimentation can help "Dream Architects" fine-tune their visual strategies to maximize vivid recall and explore the fascinating world of their own personalized dreamscapes.

Sensory Cues: Building a Multi-Sensory Dream Stage - Auditory Symphony

Sound, often overlooked in sleep hygiene, can powerfully influence our dreamscapes. Just as we can use light to subtly guide visual themes, strategic auditory cues can prime the brain for immersive, sound-rich dream recall:

1. Silence as a Foundation: Quiet the Internal Chatter

- Minimizing External Noise: A quiet sleep environment is crucial. Use earplugs, white noise machines, or sound-dampening curtains to block distracting city sounds, traffic, or noisy neighbors.

- Inner Calm through Sound: Guided meditations or sleep-focused ASMR (Autonomous Sensory Meridian Response) audio can help calm the mind, reduce racing thoughts, and transition smoothly into sleep.

2. White Noise: The Ambient Blanket for Sleep

- Constant, Steady Soundscapes: White noise (consistent, broadband sound) masks disruptive noises while creating a sense of auditory security. Use machines specifically designed for sleep, offering various sounds:

- Nature Sounds: Rain, ocean waves, forest ambience – these evoke tranquility and relaxation, potentially influencing dream themes toward nature scenes.

- Fan Noise: Classic, effective, and readily available. Provides a gentle, consistent sound to block distractions.

3. Binaural Beats: Brainwave Entrainment for Deeper Sleep

- Frequency Magic: Binaural beats are auditory illusions created by playing slightly different frequencies in each ear. These frequencies can entrain brainwaves, potentially inducing deeper sleep stages associated with vivid dreaming.

- Specific Frequencies for Specific Goals: Research suggests

    - Delta (0.5-4 Hz) for deep sleep and dream recall.

    - Theta (4-8 Hz) for relaxation, creativity, and memory consolidation

    - Experiment with binaural beat apps or recordings to find what works best for you.

4. Subliminal Auditory Cues: Whispered Words for Dream Influence

- Planting Seeds in the Subconscious:

Whispered affirmations, keywords, or phrases related to desired dream themes (e.g., "creative solutions," "past travel memories," "emotional healing") played faintly during sleep onset. The theory is that these subconscious messages might subtly influence dream content.

- Caution and Experimentation: Keep volume VERY low, and be mindful of potential for interference with sleep quality if too stimulating.

5. Dream-Enhancing Music: Setting the Sonic Stage

- Pre-Sleep Soundtrack: Listening to calming, instrumental music (classical, ambient, nature sounds) for an hour before sleep can induce relaxation and potentially imprint melodies or themes onto the dreaming brain.

- Dream-Themed Compositions: Some composers create music specifically designed to induce vivid dreams or explore particular themes. Explore these options for guided sonic exploration.

Remember: Auditory cues should complement, not dominate. The goal is to create a harmonious soundscape that supports deep sleep and enhances dream recall, not to actively "program" dreams.

Aromatherapy & Smell Memory: Unlocking Dreams with Scent Cues

Our sense of smell possesses a unique and profound ability to unlock hidden memories and emotions, unlike any other sensory modality. It's a direct pathway to the limbic system, the brain's emotional and memory center. This intimate connection makes aromatherapy a captivating tool for "Dream Architects" seeking to subtly influence their nightly journeys, potentially guiding them towards vivid recall, forgotten experiences, or even sparks of creative inspiration.

The science behind scent's influence on memory is fascinating. Unlike other senses, odor molecules bypass the usual sensory processing pathways and journey directly to the olfactory bulb, a structure nestled deep within the brain. This olfactory bulb is directly connected to the amygdala, the brain's emotional center, and the hippocampus, responsible for memory formation. This unique anatomical arrangement explains why a single whiff of a particular fragrance can instantly transport us back to a forgotten childhood memory, a beloved place, or evoke a long-dormant emotion with startling clarity. This phenomenon, aptly named the "Proustian Effect" after Marcel Proust's evocative novel "In Search of Lost Time," underscores the remarkable power of smell to trigger vivid, visceral recollections.

Harnessing this olfactory magic, we can strategically incorporate essential oils into our sleep environment to gently guide our dreamscapes. Imagine crafting a "Dream Scent Library," a personalized collection of aromatic companions, each carefully chosen to evoke specific themes or moods within the dreamscape.

Calming oils like lavender and chamomile, renowned for their sleep-promoting qualities, can weave a tranquil cocoon around your slumber, potentially deepening sleep stages associated with vivid dreaming. For those seeking to amplify memory recall, consider rosemary, known to stimulate mental clarity and focus, or peppermint, which invigorates the mind and might promote alertness and dream vividness.

But the possibilities extend beyond basic relaxation and focus. To infuse specific themes into your dreams, consider these evocative choices:

- Nature's Embrace: Pine needles, with their earthy, woodsy aroma, conjure images of serene forests, babbling brooks, and fresh mountain air, potentially guiding dreams toward outdoor adventures or moments of tranquility.

- Nostalgia's Warmth: Vanilla, with its sweet, comforting scent, often evokes childhood memories of baking, warm hugs, and cozy evenings. Diffusing vanilla oil before sleep might gently nudge your dreams toward nostalgic scenes, heartwarming encounters, or a sense of gentle contentment.

- Creative Spark: Citrus fruits like orange or lemon are known to uplift and invigorate the mind, potentially promoting creative problem-solving and unconventional dream imagery.

Instead of simply diffusing oils randomly, create a system of association. Label each bottle clearly in your "Dream Scent Library," pairing specific scents with desired themes. Experiment with timed diffusers to release aromas gradually throughout the night, allowing their subtle influence to weave through your dreamscape.

Remember, aromatherapy is a delicate art, not a forceful manipulation of dreams. Choose high-quality, pure essential oils, test for sensitivities beforehand, and avoid overwhelming scents that might disrupt sleep. Combine aromatherapy with other sleep hygiene practices, such as a dark, quiet room and soothing white noise, for a holistic approach to dream enhancement. Through mindful scent selection and diffusion, you can cultivate an aromatic sanctuary that invites vivid dreams, unlocks forgotten memories, and allows your subconscious to express itself in richer, more evocative ways.

Navigating Scent with Care: Cautions and Considerations

While aromatherapy offers a fascinating avenue for dream exploration, it's crucial to approach it with mindfulness and respect for individual sensitivities. Remember, essential oils are potent substances, and even natural products can have unforeseen effects. As you explore the world of aromatherapy, it's essential to approach it with a mindful and respectful attitude. Essential oils are highly concentrated plant extracts that can have powerful effects on the body and mind. While they can be incredibly beneficial, they can also cause adverse reactions in some individuals. It's crucial to respect individual sensitivities and approach aromatherapy with caution. Always dilute essential oils in a carrier oil before applying them to the skin, and start with small amounts to test for any adverse reactions. Be mindful of the potential interactions with medications or health conditions, and consult with a healthcare professional if you have any concerns.

Here's a guide to navigating aromatherapy safely and effectively for dream enhancement:

1. Purity Matters: Choose Quality Oils

Opt for pure, therapeutic-grade essential oils from reputable brands. Avoid synthetic fragrances or oils diluted with fillers, as they may lack efficacy and could potentially irritate skin or airways. Look for labels specifying organic sourcing and steam distillation methods, ensuring the oils are free from pesticides or harmful contaminants. When selecting essential oils, it's crucial to choose high-quality, pure oils that are safe and effective.

Reputable brands use organic sourcing methods, ensuring that the plants are grown without pesticides or other harmful chemicals. Steam distillation is a preferred method of extraction, as it preserves the delicate properties of the oils.

Avoid synthetic fragrances or oils diluted with fillers, as they can lack efficacy and potentially irritate skin or airways. Instead, opt for pure, therapeutic-grade essential oils that are free from contaminants and additives. Always check the label for organic sourcing and steam distillation methods to ensure the oils are of high quality.

2. Sensitivity First: Test Before Full-Scale Use

Every individual reacts to scents differently. Before diffusing an oil near your bed nightly, do a patch test. Apply a tiny amount diluted in a carrier oil (like almond or jojoba oil) to your inner wrist and wait 24 hours to observe for any irritation, redness, or allergic reactions. Patch testing is a crucial step in ensuring your safety and comfort when using essential oils.

By applying a small amount of the oil to your

skin and waiting for 24 hours, you can observe any potential reactions or sensitivities. This allows you to take necessary precautions and avoid any adverse effects.

When patch testing, make sure to dilute the essential oil in a carrier oil, as undiluted essential oils can be too potent for the skin. Apply a small amount to your inner wrist, cover it with a bandage, and wait for 24 hours. If you experience any irritation, redness, or allergic reactions, discontinue use and consult with a healthcare professional.

3. Dilution is Key: Avoid Overpowering Scents

Essential oils are potent. Never diffuse them undiluted. Always follow the manufacturer's instructions or guidelines for safe dilution ratios (typically 2-4 drops per 100 ml of water in a diffuser). Start with lower dilutions and gradually increase as needed. Overwhelming scents can disrupt sleep, trigger headaches, or even induce nausea.

Essential oils are highly concentrated plant extracts that can be overwhelming if not used properly. Diffusing undiluted essential oils can lead to a range of negative effects, from disrupted sleep and headaches to nausea and respiratory issues. To avoid these issues, it's crucial to dilute essential oils in water before diffusing them.

The recommended dilution ratio is typically 2-4

drops of essential oil per 100 ml of water in a diffuser. Start with lower dilutions and gradually increase as needed, taking care not to overwhelm your senses. Always follow the manufacturer's instructions and guidelines for safe dilution ratios, and consult with a healthcare professional if you have any concerns.

4. Timing is Crucial: Avoid Diffusion Too Close to Bedtime

Diffuse scents for 1-2 hours before bedtime, allowing time for the aroma to permeate the room without directly stimulating your senses immediately before sleep. If you experience restless sleep or vivid dreams that feel unsettling, adjust the diffusion duration or timing.

Diffusing scents before bed can help create a relaxing atmosphere, promoting a good night's sleep. However, it's essential to diffuse the scents at the right time to avoid stimulating your senses immediately before sleep. Diffusing scents 1-2 hours before bedtime allows the aroma to permeate the room, creating a calming atmosphere without directly stimulating your senses.

If you experience restless sleep or vivid dreams that feel unsettling, adjust the diffusion duration or timing. You may need to diffuse the scents for a shorter period or earlier in the evening to avoid stimulating your senses before sleep. Experiment with different diffusion times to find what works best for you.

5. Pregnancy and Health Considerations

Pregnant women and individuals with medical conditions (e.g., epilepsy, respiratory issues) should consult with their doctor before using essential oils. Some oils can have contraindications or interact with medications. Keep essential oils out of reach of children and pets, as they can be easily ingested and potentially harmful if not used safely.

It's crucial to exercise caution when using essential oils, especially for vulnerable populations like pregnant women, individuals with medical conditions, children, and pets. Certain essential oils can have contraindications or interact with medications, which can lead to adverse effects. For example, some essential oils can stimulate the uterus, which can be dangerous for pregnant women. Others can exacerbate respiratory issues or interact with epilepsy medications.

Always keep essential oils out of reach of children and pets, as they can be easily ingested and potentially harmful if not used safely. If you have pets, make sure to research pet-friendly essential oils and use them with caution. If you're pregnant or have a medical condition, consult with your doctor before using essential oils. They can help you determine which oils are safe for you to use and provide guidance on proper usage.

6. Respect Your Body's Signals: Listen and Adapt

Pay attention to how your body responds to each scent. If you experience headaches, dizziness, or any discomfort, discontinue use immediately and consult with a healthcare professional if needed. Dream recall is individual and not guaranteed. Aromatherapy is a subtle tool that can support your sleep environment, but it's not a magic solution for everyone. Be patient, experiment with different oils, and find what works best for you.

As you explore the world of aromatherapy, remember to approach it with awareness and respect for your body's unique needs. Pay attention to how you respond to each scent, and discontinue use if you experience any discomfort or adverse reactions. Aromatherapy is not a one-size-fits-all solution, and what works for others may not work for you.

Dream recall is individual and not guaranteed, so be patient and experiment with different oils to find what works best for you. Aromatherapy is a subtle tool that can support your sleep environment, but it's not a magic solution for everyone. By approaching aromatherapy with awareness, respect, and a focus on your well-being, you can unlock its potential to enhance your dream experiences and unlock the hidden world of olfactory memory within your nighttime adventures.

Tactile & Temperature: Crafting a Dreamscape Through Comfort

We often focus on the visual and auditory elements of sleep, envisioning calming soundscapes and softly lit rooms. However, our sense of touch, often underestimated, holds immense power in shaping the quality of our slumber and, consequently, the vividness of our dreams. Temperature and texture weave subtle threads into the fabric of our dreamscapes, influencing brainwave patterns, relaxation levels, and even the themes that emerge in our nightly adventures. "Dream Architects" can leverage this often-overlooked dimension to transform their beds into personalized sanctuaries, subtly guiding their journeys toward deeper, more immersive experiences.

Think beyond the purely functional realm of a bed as a mere resting place. Imagine it as a canvas upon which you can paint a dreamscape through tactile cues. The materials you embrace, the weight you willingly surrender to, the gentle pressure applied—these become subtle brushstrokes, shaping the contours of your subconscious explorations.

Consider the power of temperature: as your body drifts into sleep, it naturally cools, seeking a state of optimal rest. Maintaining a slightly cool bedroom temperature, around 65 degrees Fahrenheit (18 degrees Celsius), fosters deeper sleep cycles, often associated with vivid dreaming. But temperature goes beyond the overall room ambiance. Explore how specific tactile elements —weighted blankets, cooling bedding, even textured surfaces—can further influence your sleep environment and, in turn, your dreams.

From gentle pressure to the softness of materials against your skin, these seemingly mundane sensations become potent tools for guiding your subconscious into richer, more evocative nocturnal adventures.

Temperature as a Guiding Force: The Embrace of Optimal Warmth

Temperature regulation is a fundamental aspect of sleep, profoundly influencing the quality of rest and, in turn, the vividness of our dreams. While a cool overall bedroom environment (around 65 degrees Fahrenheit, or 18 degrees Celsius) is generally considered ideal, it's the nuances of tactile warmth and cooling sensations within your immediate sleep space that can truly elevate your dreamscape.

Think of your body's natural temperature fluctuations as a roadmap to deeper sleep. As you drift off, your core temperature naturally dips slightly, signaling to your brain that it's time to surrender to slumber. This cooling phase is crucial for the consolidation of memories and the emergence of vivid, dream-filled stages. By strategically manipulating localized warmth and coolness within your bed, you can amplify this natural process, subtly guiding your body and mind toward deeper, more restorative rest.

Beyond room temperature, consider these tactile nuances to harness the power of warmth (and its absence) for dream enhancement:

1. Weighted Blankets: A Soothing Embrace of Deep Pressure Stimulation: Weighted blankets provide a unique sensation – gentle, even pressure that envelops your entire body. This deep pressure stimulation has a calming effect, mimicking the feeling of a hug, reducing anxiety, and promoting feelings of security. It encourages the release of serotonin and dopamine, neurochemicals associated with relaxation and well-being, potentially leading to smoother transitions into sleep and richer dream experiences. Weighted blankets have gained popularity for their ability to provide a sense of comfort and security, similar to a warm hug. The deep pressure stimulation caused by the weighted blanket has a calming effect on the body, reducing anxiety and promoting relaxation. This

is due to the release of serotonin and dopamine, neurochemicals associated with feelings of well-being and relaxation. The weighted blanket's gentle pressure also helps to reduce stress and anxiety, making it easier to fall asleep and stay asleep. Additionally, the weighted blanket can help to increase the production of melatonin, the hormone responsible for regulating sleep-wake cycles. This can lead to richer dream experiences and improved overall sleep quality.

2. Cooling Textiles: Breathing Easy for Optimal Rest: Breathable, natural fibers like cotton, linen, or bamboo are your allies in regulating temperature. They allow air to circulate freely, preventing overheating and restless sleep that can disrupt dream cycles. Imagine sinking into sheets that feel like a cool, gentle caress against your skin, facilitating a consistent temperature throughout the night. Breathable textiles are essential for a restful night's sleep. Natural fibers like cotton, linen, or bamboo allow air to circulate freely, preventing overheating and promoting a consistent temperature throughout the night. This helps regulate your body temperature, ensuring that you stay cool and comfortable, even during the

hottest summer nights. Imagine sinking into sheets that feel like a cool, gentle caress against your skin. The breathability of the textiles ensures that you stay comfortable, without feeling too hot or too cold. This helps promote a restful night's sleep, allowing you to wake up feeling refreshed and rejuvenated. By choosing breathable textiles, you can create a sleep environment that promotes comfort, relaxation, and restful sleep.

3. Temperature-Regulating Mattress Pads: Tailoring Comfort for Deeper Sleep: If you tend to sleep hot, invest in a cooling mattress pad infused with gel, memory foam with phase-change materials, or breathable materials that dissipate heat effectively. This targeted cooling can create a consistent, sleep-conducive surface temperature, preventing those restless nighttime shifts and potentially enhancing the continuity and vividness of your dreams. Temperature-regulating mattress pads are designed to provide a comfortable sleeping surface by maintaining a consistent temperature. For those who tend to sleep hot, cooling mattress pads infused with gel, memory foam with phase-change materials, or breathable materials can dissipate heat effectively.

This targeted cooling can prevent restless nighttime shifts, allowing for deeper and more restful sleep. The consistent surface temperature created by temperature-regulating mattress pads can also enhance the continuity and vividness of dreams. By providing a comfortable sleeping surface, these mattress pads can promote deeper sleep and increase the likelihood of remembering dreams. Additionally, the reduced tossing and turning can lead to better sleep quality, which can also contribute to more vivid and memorable dreams.

Remember, temperature is a subtle guide, not a forceful dictator. Experiment with different combinations of weighted blankets, cooling textiles, and mattress toppers to discover your ideal sleep temperature sweet spot. Over time, you'll learn how to create a personalized haven of comfort that nurtures restful sleep and unlocks the full potential of your dream landscapes.

Temperature is a crucial aspect of creating a sleep-conducive environment, but it's essential to approach it with subtlety. Rather than trying to force a specific temperature, experiment with different combinations of weighted blankets, cooling textiles, and mattress toppers to find your ideal sleep temperature sweet spot.

This may take some trial and error, but over time, you'll learn how to create a personalized haven of comfort that nurtures restful sleep and unlocks the full potential of your dream landscapes. Remember, the key is to find a temperature that makes you feel comfortable and relaxed, allowing you to sink into a deep and restorative sleep. By experimenting with different temperature combinations, you can create a sleep environment that is tailored to your unique needs, promoting better sleep and more vivid dreams.

Beyond the Physical: Mindset and Intention – The Power of Belief

While crafting the ideal sleep environment with soothing sounds, calming scents, and comfortable textures is essential, remember that the most potent ingredient for vivid dream recall lies within yourself: your mindset and intention.

Creating a sleep-conducive environment is crucial for promoting vivid dream recall, but it's only half the equation. The other half lies within your own mindset and intention. Your ability to recall dreams vividly depends on your mental attitude and willingness to tap into your subconscious mind.

By cultivating a mindset that values dream recall and exploration, you can unlock the full potential of your dreams. This means being intentional about remembering your dreams, keeping a dream journal, and practicing techniques like reality checking and meditation to increase your self-awareness.

Remember, the power to recall vivid dreams lies within you. By combining a sleep-conducive environment with a mindset that values dream exploration, you can unlock the secrets of your subconscious mind and tap into the rich world of your dreams.

Think of your dream recall journey not just as a technical exercise in sensory optimization, but as a conscious act of will, a gentle nudge toward conscious dreaming. By cultivating a specific mindset and directing your intentions before sleep, you can empower your subconscious mind to weave richer, more memorable dreamscapes.

Your dream recall journey is not just about optimizing your sleep environment or using techniques to improve recall. It's also about cultivating a specific mindset that empowers your subconscious mind to create richer, more memorable dreamscapes. By directing your intentions before sleep, you can nudge your subconscious mind toward conscious dreaming, allowing you to tap into the full potential of your dreams.

This mindset involves being open to the possibilities of your subconscious mind, trusting in its ability to create meaningful and memorable dreams. It also involves being intentional about your dreams, directing your subconscious mind toward specific themes or topics that you want to explore. By cultivating this mindset and directing your intentions, you can empower your subconscious mind to weave richer, more memorable dreamscapes that can help you tap into the full potential of your dreams.

Cultivating the Belief: Embrace the Power of Expectation

The human mind is not a passive recipient of information; it's a powerful sculptor, shaping our experiences based on our beliefs and expectations. When it comes to dream recall, this holds immense significance. If you consciously believe that you'll remember your dreams vividly, you prime your brain to pay closer attention to them upon waking. This isn't simply wishful thinking; it taps into the remarkable neuroplasticity of the brain, its ability to rewire itself based on our focus and intent.

The mind plays a crucial role in shaping our experiences, including dream recall. By believing that you'll remember your dreams vividly, you prime your brain to pay closer attention to them upon waking. This belief taps into the neuroplasticity of the brain, allowing it to rewire itself based on your focus and intent.

Neuroplasticity is the brain's ability to adapt and change in response to new experiences and information. By focusing your intent on remembering your dreams, you can rewire your brain to prioritize dream recall. This can lead to improved dream recall, allowing you to tap into the subconscious mind and access the hidden world of your dreams.

Think of belief as a fertile ground for dream vividness to sprout. Before sleep, engage in mental rehearsal, vividly visualizing yourself recalling dream details with clarity. Imagine waking up with a sense of excitement, effortlessly recalling characters, emotions, and storylines with vivid detail. Don't just passively hope for vivid dreams; actively construct a mental narrative of successful recall.

Belief plays a crucial role in cultivating vivid dreams. Before sleep, engage in mental rehearsal, vividly visualizing yourself recalling dream details with clarity. Imagine waking up with a sense of excitement, effortlessly recalling characters, emotions, and storylines with vivid detail. This mental rehearsal helps to construct a mental narrative of successful recall, empowering your subconscious mind to create more vivid and memorable dreams.

By actively visualizing yourself recalling dream details, you can tap into the power of your subconscious mind and unlock the full potential of your dreams. This mental rehearsal can help to increase your self-awareness, allowing you to better navigate your dreams and recall them with greater clarity. Remember, the key to vivid dreams lies within your own mind. By believing in your ability to recall your dreams and actively visualizing success, you can unlock the full potential of your subconscious mind and tap into the world of your dreams.

Here's how to cultivate this empowering belief:

1. Affirmations: Reframing Your Internal Dialogue: Incorporate positive affirmations into your bedtime routine. Instead of "I hope I remember my dreams," declare, "My dreams are vivid and memorable." Repeat these affirmations with conviction, allowing them to sink deep into your subconscious. Positive affirmations can help reframe your internal dialogue, replacing negative self-talk with empowering statements that promote confidence and self-belief. By incorporating affirmations into your bedtime routine, you can cultivate a positive mindset that supports vivid dream recall. Instead of

saying "I hope I remember my dreams," try declaring "My dreams are vivid and memorable." Repeat this affirmation with conviction, allowing it to sink deep into your subconscious. This helps to rewire your brain with positive thoughts and beliefs, promoting a mindset that supports vivid dream recall. Remember to repeat your affirmations regularly, especially before sleep, to maximize their effectiveness.

2. Dream Recall Success Stories: Harnessing the Power of Social Proof: Read accounts of others who vividly recall their dreams. Hearing compelling stories of lucid dreaming or detailed dream experiences can reinforce your belief that it's achievable for you as well. This exposure to "success stories" can inspire and motivate you. Reading accounts of others who vividly recall their dreams can be a powerful motivator. Hearing compelling stories of lucid dreaming or detailed dream experiences can reinforce your belief that it's achievable for you as well. This exposure to "success stories" can inspire and motivate you to work towards improving your own dream recall. By reading about others' experiences, you can gain valuable insights and tips on how to improve

your own dream recall. You can learn about different techniques and strategies that have worked for others, and try them out for yourself. Additionally, reading about others' success stories can help to build your confidence and motivation, encouraging you to continue working towards your goal of improving your dream recall.

3. Focus on the Positive: Amplifying the Signals of Recall: When you do remember a dream, no matter how small, savor it fully. Engage all your senses in reliving the experience. This reinforces neural pathways associated with dream memory, strengthening your ability to recall future dreams. When you remember a dream, no matter how small, savor it fully. Engage all your senses in reliving the experience, from the sights and sounds to the emotions and sensations. This helps to reinforce neural pathways associated with dream memory, strengthening your ability to recall future dreams. By focusing on the positive experience of remembering a dream, you can amplify the signals of recall in your brain. This can help to strengthen your ability to remember dreams and improve your overall dream recall. Additionally, savoring the experience of remembering a

dream can help to increase your motivation and enthusiasm for dream recall, leading to a positive feedback loop that can help you achieve your goals.

4. Visualization: Mentally Rehearse Dream Recall: As you lie in bed, visualize yourself waking up, feeling refreshed, and effortlessly recounting your dream. See yourself jotting down details in your journal with clarity and enthusiasm. This mental rehearsal creates a powerful expectation for vivid recall. Visualization is a powerful tool for mental rehearsal, allowing you to mentally practice and prepare for dream recall. As you lie in bed, visualize yourself waking up feeling refreshed and effortlessly recounting your dream. See yourself jotting down details in your journal with clarity and enthusiasm. This mental rehearsal creates a powerful expectation for vivid recall, programming your mind to prioritize dream recall and strengthening your ability to remember your dreams. By visualizing yourself successfully recalling your dreams, you can build confidence and motivation, leading to improved dream recall over time. Remember to be specific and detailed in your visualization, imagining yourself recalling specific details and emotions from

your dreams.

Remember, belief is not simply wishful thinking; it's a conscious choice that can profoundly influence your dream recall. By choosing to believe in your ability to recall your dreams, you can tap into the power of your subconscious mind and unlock the full potential of your dreams. Belief is not just a passive state of mind; it's an active choice that can shape your reality.

By choosing to believe in your ability to recall your dreams, you can create a positive feedback loop that reinforces your confidence and motivation. This can lead to improved dream recall, as your subconscious mind responds to your positive beliefs and expectations. Remember, your beliefs have the power to shape your reality. By choosing to believe in your ability to recall your dreams, you can unlock the full potential of your subconscious mind and tap into the rich world of your dreams.

Dream Journaling: A Bridge Between Slumber and Awareness

Beyond its role as a repository of nocturnal adventures, your dream journal becomes a potent tool for intention-setting, memory enhancement, and deepening your connection to your subconscious. It's a physical manifestation of your commitment to conscious dreaming, bridging the gap between the world of sleep and the waking realm.

Think of your dream journal not merely as a passive recorder, but as an active participant in your dream exploration. It's a space where you can engage in dialogue with your sleeping mind, offering guidance, prompting recall, and even planting seeds of intention for richer, more evocative dreamscapes.

1. Crafting a Sensory Sanctuary: Choose a journal that invites you to dive deep. Opt for a journal with creamy paper that feels delightful against your fingertips, perhaps with a scent that evokes calm and creativity, like lavender or vanilla. Keep it close to your bed, a welcoming companion within arm's reach when you wake.

2. Beyond Chronological Entries: Embrace the Art of Descriptive Recall: Don't simply jot down fragmented fragments; strive for sensory richness. Capture not just the storyline but also the textures, sounds, smells, and emotions you experienced.

- "I drifted through a forest where the leaves rustled like whispers, their emerald green blending with the scent of damp earth."
- "A character's laughter echoed with a metallic tang, like wind chimes struck by unseen hands."
- This vivid detail strengthens

neural pathways associated with memory, enhancing your ability to recall dreams with clarity.

3. Intention Setting: Planting Seeds for Nightly Adventures: Before sleep, take a moment to pen your dreamscapes desires. Do you crave adventure, emotional exploration, or perhaps revisiting a forgotten memory? Write these intentions as affirmations: "Tonight, I will dream of soaring through skies painted with vibrant hues," or "I will explore the forgotten emotions nestled within my subconscious." This act of pre-sleep intention setting subtly guides your subconscious, subtly influencing the themes and content of your dreams.

4. Lucid Dreaming Prompts: Guiding Consciousness Within Dreams:

Incorporate specific prompts to encourage lucid dreaming (awareness within dreams). Write: "Tonight, I will remember I am dreaming" or "I will notice any inconsistencies in my dream world." These cues can act as mental anchors, increasing your chances of recognizing yourself within a dream and gaining conscious control.

Morning Review: Reinforcing the Connection Between Dream and Waking World: Even if you only remember fragments, review your journal each morning. Connecting with your dreams upon waking strengthens the neural pathways associated with recall. Look for recurring themes, emotional patterns, or symbols – these can offer valuable insights into your subconscious mind.

Remember: Dream journaling is a journey, not a destination. Be patient with yourself, approach it with curiosity, and allow it to become a cherished ritual, deepening your connection to the rich and mysterious world of dreams.

Lucid Dreaming Techniques: A Conscious Journey Within Dreams

Lucid dreaming, the extraordinary ability to become aware that you are dreaming while still within the dream itself, is not merely a fantastical notion. It's a state of heightened consciousness achievable through dedicated practice and specific techniques.

Imagine stepping beyond the passive role of a dreamer and consciously shaping your nocturnal landscapes, interacting with dream characters, exploring impossible scenarios, or even revisiting cherished memories in vivid detail. Lucid dreaming empowers you to become the director of your own dream world, transforming slumber into a realm of creative exploration and self-discovery. And though the dreamer remains asleep, he walks through memory as if experiencing it for the first time anew, no longer a passenger but an active participant.

Here are some key techniques to embark on this conscious journey within your dreams:

1. Reality Checks: Establishing a Waking World Anchor:

Throughout your day, perform regular reality checks. Pause several times an hour and ask yourself, "Am I dreaming?" Examine your surroundings for inconsistencies – do objects look distorted? Are your hands solid or transparent? Can you read text clearly? These checks create a habit of questioning your reality, which carries over into dreams, potentially triggering lucidity when you encounter illogical elements within your dream environment. Reality checking is a powerful technique for cultivating lucidity in dreams.

By regularly questioning your reality during the day, you create a habit that can carry over into your dreams. This can help you become more aware of your surroundings and more likely to notice illogical elements that can trigger lucidity. To perform reality checks, pause several times an hour and ask yourself, "Am I dreaming?"

Examine your surroundings for inconsistencies, such as distorted objects, transparent hands, or unclear text. You can also perform physical reality checks, such as pinching yourself or looking at your hands to see if they are solid. By incorporating reality checks into your daily routine, you can cultivate a habit of questioning your reality that can help you achieve lucidity in your dreams.

2. Mnemonic Induction of Lucid Dreams (MILD): Planting the Seed of Awareness:

As you drift off to sleep, visualize yourself becoming lucid within a dream. Repeatedly repeat a phrase like, "I will know I am dreaming" or "I will become lucid in my next dream" with conviction. Picture yourself waking up within a dream, recognizing it as a dream state with clarity. MILD strengthens the neural pathways associated with lucid dreaming, increasing your chances of awakening within your dream. MILD (Mnemonic Induction of Lucid Dreams) is a powerful technique for inducing lucid dreaming.

By visualizing yourself becoming lucid within a dream and repeating a mantra-like phrase, you can strengthen the neural pathways associated with lucid dreaming. This increases your chances of awakening within your dream and becoming lucid. To practice MILD, visualize yourself becoming lucid within a dream. Picture yourself recognizing the dream state with clarity and taking control of your actions. Repeat a phrase like, "I will know I am dreaming" or "I will become lucid in my next dream" with conviction.

This helps to program your mind to recognize the dream state and become lucid. By practicing MILD regularly, you can increase your chances of having a lucid dream and exploring the vast possibilities of your subconscious mind.

3. Wake Back to Bed (WBTB): Harnessing the Power of Interrupted Sleep:

Set an alarm to wake you up after 5-6 hours of sleep. Stay awake for 20-30 minutes, focusing on lucid dreaming intentions, reading about lucid dreaming, or performing reality checks. Then, return to sleep with a heightened awareness of your dream potential. This technique takes advantage of the heightened REM activity during the subsequent sleep cycle, increasing your chances of entering a lucid dream. This technique, known as the "wake-back-to-bed" method, involves setting an alarm to wake you up after 5-6 hours of sleep.

You then stay awake for 20-30 minutes, focusing on lucid dreaming intentions, reading about lucid dreaming, or performing reality checks. This helps to increase your awareness of your dream potential and primes your mind for lucid dreaming. After 20-30 minutes, you return to sleep with a heightened awareness of your dream potential. This technique takes advantage of the heightened REM activity during the subsequent sleep cycle, increasing your chances of entering a lucid dream.

By waking up and staying awake for a short period, you can increase your self-awareness and improve your ability to recognize when you are dreaming, making it easier to enter a lucid dream state.

4. Dream Signs: Recognizing Personal Clues:

Pay attention to recurring symbols or patterns in your dreams. A specific object, location, or emotion might consistently signal a dream state. As you become aware of these personal "dream signs," you can use them as triggers for lucidity within your dreams. Dream signs are personal symbols or patterns that appear in your dreams and can serve as triggers for lucidity. By paying attention to recurring symbols or patterns in your dreams, you can identify your personal dream signs and use them to increase your self-awareness within dreams.

Common dream signs include specific objects, locations, emotions, or sensations that appear frequently in your dreams. For example, you might notice that you often dream about a particular place from your childhood or that you frequently experience a sense of fear or anxiety in your dreams. By recognizing these dream signs, you can use them as triggers for lucidity, reminding yourself to become more aware and take control of your dreams.

5. Dream Journaling as a Gateway to Awareness:

Thorough dream recall, even of fragmented dreams, strengthens your dream memory and creates a framework for recognizing familiar patterns and recurring themes. This heightened awareness can facilitate lucid dreaming as you begin to recognize your dreamscape elements with greater clarity.

Dream recall is essential for lucid dreaming. By strengthening your dream memory, you can create a framework for recognizing familiar patterns and recurring themes in your dreams. This heightened awareness can help you identify dream signs, which are personal symbols or patterns that appear in your dreams and can serve as triggers for lucidity.

To improve your dream recall, keep a dream journal and write down as many details as you can remember about your dreams. Even if you only remember fragments, write them down. Over time, you can review your journal and look for recurring themes and patterns. This can help you identify dream signs and improve your ability to recognize them in your dreams, leading to increased lucidity.

Remember, lucid dreaming is a skill that develops with consistent practice and patience. Be kind to yourself, celebrate small successes, and embrace the journey of expanding your dream consciousness. With dedication and exploration, you can unlock the extraordinary potential of consciously navigating your own inner worlds.

Lucid dreaming is a skill that requires consistent practice and patience to develop. It's essential to be kind to yourself and celebrate small successes along the way. Embracing the journey of expanding your dream consciousness can help you stay motivated and committed to your practice.

With dedication and exploration, you can unlock the extraordinary potential of consciously navigating your own inner worlds. Lucid dreaming allows you to tap into your subconscious mind, explore your deepest fears and desires, and gain insight into your waking life. By embracing the journey of lucid dreaming, you can unlock the secrets of your mind and discover new depths of consciousness.

Technology for Dream Architects: Tools to Enhance Your Nocturnal Adventures

While the foundation of dream enhancement lies in lifestyle changes, sound sleep hygiene, and mindful intention, technology offers fascinating tools to augment your efforts and delve deeper into the realm of conscious dreaming. Here are some innovative gadgets and digital companions to empower your journey as a Dream Architect:

1. Wearable Sleep Trackers: Unlocking the Data of

Slumber

Beyond simple sleep duration tracking, modern wearables like smartwatches and fitness trackers now offer detailed insights into your sleep stages, heart rate variability, and even blood oxygen levels. This data can help you identify optimal sleep times for deeper REM cycles, potentially boosting dream recall. Some devices even feature gentle alarms that wake you during lighter sleep phases, minimizing grogginess and potentially increasing chances of remembering dreams.

Dream Recall-Focused Apps: Apps like Sleep Cycle, Dream Journal, or Pillow analyze your sleep patterns and wake you at ideal moments for dream recall, often accompanied by gentle sounds or vibrations that encourage waking consciousness.

2. Sensory Stimulation Devices: Guiding Dreamscapes with Gentle Enchantment

Weighted Blankets with Built-in Soundscapes: Combine the comforting pressure of a weighted blanket with soothing ambient sounds, nature noises, or binaural beats designed to promote relaxation and potentially influence dream content.

Dream Light Projector: These devices project calming, rotating patterns or mesmerizing visuals onto your ceiling, creating a subtle yet engaging sensory experience before sleep. Choose patterns known to induce relaxation or evoke desired dream themes, like forests, starry skies, or abstract art.

3. Brainwave Entrainment Devices: Tuning Your Brainwaves for Dream Enhancement

Neurotech gadgets like binaural beat headphones or light therapy devices utilize specific frequencies to gently influence brainwave patterns. While not directly "programming" dreams, they can nudge you towards deeper sleep stages or promote alpha and theta brainwaves associated with creativity and dream recall.

Caution: Research into direct impact on dream content is still evolving, so proceed with careful consideration and consult with healthcare professionals if you have concerns.

4. Voice-Activated Dream Recall Assistants:

Imagine waking up and effortlessly dictating your dreams into a device. AI-powered voice assistants like Alexa or Google Assistant, integrated with dedicated dream journaling apps, can become your bedside companions. Set a routine: "Alexa, start dream recording" upon waking. Speak your dream narrative as it emerges, capturing details as vividly as possible. This hands-free approach eliminates the cognitive effort of note-taking, potentially improving dream recall by minimizing mental barriers between waking and dreaming.

5. Augmented Reality (AR) for Dream Exploration

(Future Potential):

While still in its infancy, AR holds exciting potential for dream enhancement. Imagine overlaying interactive elements onto your waking environment, based on your dream journals.

- Dreamscape Visualizations: AR could project dream-inspired imagery onto your bedroom walls, creating a tangible link between your subconscious and physical space.
- Dream Navigation Tools: Future AR apps might allow you to "walk through" your dream landscapes virtually, reliving experiences in a richer, more immersive way.

Important Considerations:

- Remember that technology should complement, not replace, foundational sleep hygiene practices. Prioritize a regular sleep schedule, calming bedtime routines, and a conducive sleep environment.

- Be mindful of blue light exposure from devices before bed. Utilize "night mode" settings on screens to minimize melatonin suppression.

- Experiment and find what resonates best with you. Not every tech tool will be beneficial for everyone. Treat technology as a tool to enhance your innate dream potential, not a magic solution.

As technology evolves, expect even more sophisticated tools to emerge, further empowering Dream Architects to explore the fascinating realms of their own minds with increasing clarity and intention.

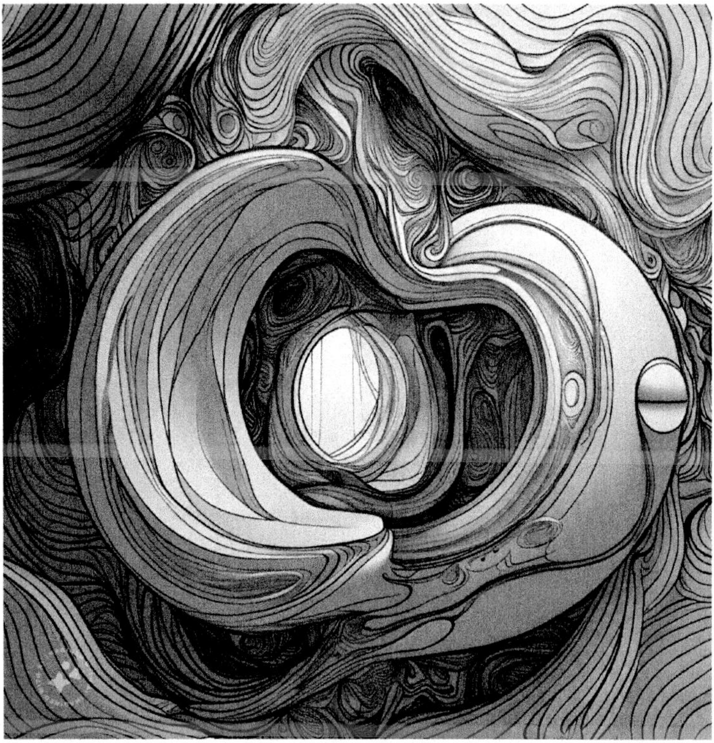

DREAM PODS AND SENSORY IMMERSION - SCULPTING YOUR DREAMSCAPE

Introduction

Imagine stepping beyond the confines of your traditional bedroom, leaving behind the mundane clutter and ambient distractions of everyday life, and entering a sanctuary meticulously designed to optimize not just your sleep, but your dreamscape itself. This is the burgeoning world of "Dream Pods" – immersive sleep chambers poised to revolutionize the way we approach rest and explore the captivating realm of our subconscious.

No longer are we confined to passively drifting into slumber within a space primarily designed for rest. Dream Pods usher in an era where sleep becomes an active pursuit, a curated journey into heightened consciousness and deeper dream recall. They are more than just beds; they're personalized environments where technology seamlessly intertwines with sensory comfort, sculpting a bespoke sleep experience tailored to individual desires.

Current iterations of this concept exist in various forms. Sleep Number, known for its innovative sleep beds, is already incorporating sensory features into its "SleepIQ" systems, incorporating adjustable firmness, temperature control, and even gentle massage functions to promote deeper sleep. Meanwhile, startups and research labs are pushing the boundaries further, prototyping more radical "pod" designs with integrated lighting, sound, and even aroma therapy systems.

This burgeoning field reflects a broader societal shift toward sleep optimization as a vital pillar of wellness. As we increasingly recognize the profound impact of sleep on our physical and mental health, the pursuit of restorative and even transformative slumber is gaining momentum. Dream Pods, with their promise of heightened dream recall, lucid dreaming potential, and personalized sensory environments, represent a fascinating frontier in this quest for optimal sleep and a deeper understanding of our own inner worlds.

Sight

Within the carefully crafted cocoon of a Dream Pod, visual stimulation becomes a potent tool, delicately shaping the landscapes of your dreams. Gone are the disruptive intrusions of blue light from screens; instead, curated visual cues become gentle companions to your descent into slumber, guiding your mind towards a realm of deeper relaxation and richer dream recall.

The foundation of this sensory immersion lies in embracing true darkness. True, enveloping blackness, devoid of streetlights filtering through blinds or the faint glow of electronic devices, allows the production of melatonin, the sleep hormone, to flourish. This hormonal shift is essential for promoting natural sleep cycles and deepening into REM sleep, the stage where vivid dreaming unfolds. Dream Pods achieve this profound darkness through meticulously designed blackout curtains, strategically positioned light-blocking panels, or even innovative materials within the pod's walls that actively absorb light, creating a sanctuary of absolute visual stillness.

But darkness alone is not enough. Dream Pods can elevate this foundation with programmable light shows designed to lull you into a dream-conducive state. Imagine a gentle symphony of visual cues unfolding as you drift off: projections of tranquil forests, star-strewn night skies, or the mesmerizing ebb and flow of ocean waves, each scene a visual lullaby transporting your mind to serene landscapes. These subtle, evolving patterns of color and form can stimulate the visual cortex without being jarring, inducing a meditative state that encourages dream emergence.

For those seeking to cultivate lucid dreaming, specific visual prompts can be woven into this tapestry of light. Imagine recurring dream symbols —perhaps keys, clocks, or doorways—appearing as soft, ephemeral projections, subtly nudging your subconscious, prompting recognition of the dream state. Complex, intricate geometric patterns, known to stimulate brain activity, might also serve as gentle triggers for heightened dream awareness.

Remember, the key is to orchestrate a visual symphony that is calming and harmonious, not overwhelming or disruptive. It's about crafting a gentle visual language that invites your mind to delve deeper, to explore the realms of your dreams with newfound clarity and intention.

Touch

The sense of touch plays a profound role in our sleep and dreaming experiences. The comfort and pressure we experience during sleep can significantly impact our ability to relax and enter a state of deep sleep, and even influence the content of our dreams. In this section, we will delve into the world of touch and explore the use of weighted blankets and haptic feedback devices to enhance our sleep and dreaming experiences.

Weighted Blankets: Deep Pressure Stimulation for Relaxation

Weighted blankets have become increasingly popular in recent years, and for good reason. These blankets use deep pressure stimulation (DPS) to provide a calming, grounding sensation that can help individuals relax and fall asleep faster. DPS works by applying gentle pressure to the body, which stimulates the production of serotonin and melatonin, two neurotransmitters that play a key role in regulating sleep and relaxation.

The use of weighted blankets has been shown to have a number of benefits, including:

- Reduced stress and anxiety: The deep pressure stimulation provided by weighted blankets can help to reduce stress and anxiety, making it easier to fall asleep and stay asleep.
- Improved sleep quality: Weighted blankets can help to improve sleep quality by providing a sense of comfort and security, which can lead to deeper and more restful sleep.
- Increased relaxation: The deep pressure stimulation provided by weighted blankets can

help to increase relaxation, which can lead to a sense of calm and well-being.

Haptic Feedback Devices: Gentle Stimulation for Enhanced Dreaming

Haptic feedback devices use subtle vibrations or gentle nudges to stimulate the skin during sleep and dreaming. These devices can be particularly beneficial for individuals who experience lucid dreaming, as they can provide a gentle reminder to become aware of their dreams and take control of the narrative. The use of haptic feedback devices has been shown to have a number of benefits,

- Increased lucid dreaming: Haptic feedback devices can help to increase the frequency and intensity of lucid dreaming, allowing individuals to take control of their dreams and explore their subconscious mind.
- Improved dream recall: Haptic feedback devices can also help to improve dream recall, allowing individuals to remember their dreams more clearly and in greater detail.
- Enhanced creativity: The use of haptic feedback devices can also enhance creativity, allowing individuals to tap into their subconscious mind and access new ideas and inspiration.

Integrating Weighted Blankets and Haptic Feedback Devices

Weighted blankets and haptic feedback devices can be integrated to create a comprehensive sleep and dreaming system. This system can provide a comfortable and supportive sleep environment, while also stimulating the mind and promoting lucid dreaming.

Benefits of Integration

The integration of weighted blankets and haptic feedback devices can provide a number of benefits, including:

- Improved sleep quality: The combination of weighted blankets and haptic feedback devices can help to improve sleep quality, leading to better rest and relaxation.

- Increased lucid dreaming: The use of haptic feedback devices can help to increase the frequency and intensity of lucid dreaming, allowing individuals to tap into their subconscious mind and access new ideas and inspiration.

- Enhanced creativity: The combination of weighted blankets and haptic feedback devices can help to enhance creativity, allowing individuals to tap into their subconscious mind and access new ideas and inspiration.

The integration of weighted blankets and haptic feedback devices can provide a comprehensive sleep and dreaming system that can help to improve sleep quality, increase lucid dreaming, and enhance creativity. By providing a comfortable and supportive sleep environment, while also stimulating the mind and promoting lucid dreaming, this system can help individuals to tap into their subconscious mind and access new ideas and inspiration.

Smell

The sense of smell is closely linked to the brain's limbic system, which is responsible for emotions, memories, and mood regulation. Aromatherapy, the practice of using essential oils to promote physical and emotional well-being, can be a powerful tool for influencing mood and dreams. In this section, we will explore the use of aromatherapy for promoting relaxation and specific dream themes, as well as the use of olfactory sensors to adjust scent intensities based on sleep stage.

Aromatherapy for Relaxation

Certain essential oils, such as lavender and chamomile, are known for their calming and relaxing properties. These oils can be used to promote relaxation and reduce stress and anxiety, making it easier to fall asleep and stay asleep. Aromatherapy can be particularly beneficial for individuals who experience insomnia or other sleep disorders.

Aromatherapy for Specific Dream Themes

In addition to promoting relaxation, aromatherapy can also be used to influence specific dream themes. Certain essential oils, such as citrus and peppermint, are known to promote energy and alertness, while others, such as sandalwood and vanilla, are known to promote relaxation and calmness. By using specific essential oils, individuals can influence the content of their dreams and promote specific themes or emotions.

Olfactory Sensors for Adjusting Scent Intensities

Olfactory sensors are devices that can detect and adjust scent intensities based on sleep stage. These devices can be particularly beneficial for individuals who experience sleep disorders or insomnia, as they can help to promote relaxation and reduce stress and anxiety. Olfactory sensors work by detecting the scent intensity of essential oils and adjusting it based on sleep stage. For example, during the light sleep stage, the scent intensity may be adjusted to promote relaxation and calmness, while during the deep sleep stage, the scent intensity may be adjusted to promote energy and alertness.

Benefits of Olfactory Sensors

The use of olfactory sensors can provide a number of benefits, including:

- Improved sleep quality: Olfactory sensors can help to promote relaxation and reduce stress and anxiety, leading to improved sleep quality.

- Increased relaxation: Olfactory sensors can help to promote relaxation and calmness, leading to increased relaxation and reduced stress and anxiety.

- Enhanced dreaming: Olfactory sensors can help to promote specific dream themes and emotions, leading to enhanced dreaming and increased creativity.

The use of aromatherapy and olfactory sensors can be a powerful tool for influencing mood and dreams. By using specific essential oils and adjusting scent intensities based on sleep stage, individuals can promote relaxation, reduce stress and anxiety, and enhance their dreaming experiences. Additionally, the use of olfactory sensors can provide a new level of control and customization over the sleep environment, allowing individuals to tailor their sleep experience to their specific needs and preferences.

Future Research Directions

While the use of aromatherapy and olfactory sensors shows promise for influencing mood and dreams, there is still much to be learned about the mechanisms by which these technologies work and the optimal ways to use them. Future research directions could include:

- Investigating the neural mechanisms by which aromatherapy and olfactory sensors influence mood and dreams

- Developing more sophisticated olfactory sensors that can detect and adjust scent intensities based on sleep stage and other factors

- Conducting larger-scale studies to investigate the efficacy of aromatherapy and olfactory sensors for promoting relaxation and enhancing dreaming experiences

- Exploring the potential applications of aromatherapy and olfactory sensors in other areas, such as anxiety and depression treatment, pain management, and cognitive enhancement

The use of aromatherapy and olfactory sensors is a promising area of research for promoting relaxation and enhancing dreaming experiences. While there is still much to be learned about the mechanisms by which these technologies work and the optimal ways to use them, the existing evidence suggests that they can be a powerful tool for improving sleep quality and promoting relaxation. As research continues to advance in this area, we can expect to see even more innovative applications of aromatherapy and olfactory sensors in the future.

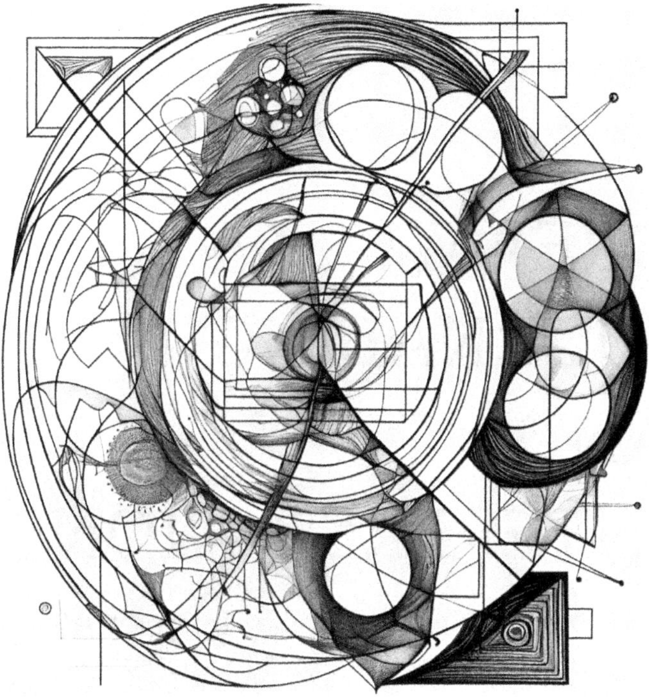

DREAM JOURNALING AND INTERPRETATION

Dream journaling and interpretation are powerful tools for tapping into the subconscious mind and gaining insight into our waking lives. By recording and analyzing our dreams, we can uncover hidden patterns, desires, and fears that can help us better understand ourselves and the world around us. This practice has been used for centuries by spiritual leaders, artists, and writers to tap into the subconscious mind and gain inspiration for their work.

The study of dreams has a long and fascinating history, with ancient cultures such as the Egyptians, Greeks, and Romans placing great significance on dreams and their ability to predict the future. In fact, the ancient Egyptians believed that dreams were a way for the gods to communicate with mortals, and they would often seek guidance from dream interpreters to help them make important decisions. Similarly, the ancient Greeks believed that dreams were a way for the subconscious mind to communicate with the conscious mind, and they would often use dream analysis as a tool for self-discovery and personal growth.

In recent years, the study of dreams has become a growing field of research, with scientists and psychologists exploring the neural mechanisms behind dreaming and the potential therapeutic applications of lucid dreaming. Lucid dreaming is the ability to consciously recognize and control one's dreams while still asleep, and it has been shown to have a number of benefits, including improved problem-solving skills, increased creativity, and reduced anxiety and stress. By studying lucid dreaming and the neural mechanisms behind it, researchers hope to gain a better understanding of the subconscious mind and how it can be harnessed for personal growth and self-improvement.

This chapter will provide practical exercises and guidance on effectively documenting dreams, identifying recurring themes, and interpreting the "playback" data gleaned from them. By the end of this chapter, readers will have the tools and techniques necessary to unlock the secrets of their dreams and tap into the hidden potential of their subconscious mind. Whether you are a seasoned dreamer or just starting out, this chapter will provide you with the knowledge and skills necessary to take your dream practice to the next level and unlock the full potential of your subconscious mind.

Setting Up Your Dream Journal

Setting up a dream journal is a crucial step in cultivating a deeper understanding of your subconscious mind and unlocking the secrets of your dreams. A dream journal is a dedicated space where you can record your dreams, thoughts, and feelings, and it serves as a powerful tool for tracking your progress, identifying recurring themes, and gaining insight into your waking life.

Choosing the Right Journal

When it comes to selecting a dream journal, there are several factors to consider. First and foremost, choose a journal that feels comfortable and inviting to you. Consider the size, shape, and weight of the journal, as well as the type of paper and binding. Do you prefer a journal with a soft cover or a hardcover? Do you like the feel of lined paper or blank paper? These may seem like trivial details, but they can make a big difference in your overall experience. Another important consideration is the journal's durability.

You'll want a journal that can withstand regular use and handling, as well as the occasional accidental drop or spill. Look for a journal with high-quality paper and binding, and consider investing in a journal with a waterproof cover or a built-in elastic closure. Setting Up Your Journal

Once you've chosen your dream journal, it's time to set it up. Start by writing your name and the date on the inside cover, and then take a few moments to reflect on your intentions for using the journal. What do you hope to achieve through dream journaling? What themes or patterns do you hope to explore? Next, create an index or table of contents to help you keep track of your entries. You can use a simple numerical system, or create a more elaborate index with categories and subcategories. Finally, take a few moments to decorate your journal with images, symbols, or other embellishments that resonate with you.

Making Dream Journaling a Habit

The key to successful dream journaling is consistency. Make a commitment to yourself to journal every day, even if it's just for a few minutes. Start by setting aside a specific time and place for journaling, such as first thing in the morning or before bed. Then, create a ritual around journaling, such as lighting a candle or sipping a cup of tea. As you journal, remember to be patient and kind to yourself. Don't worry if your entries seem fragmented or disjointed – the goal is to capture your thoughts and feelings, not to create

Recording Your Dreams

Recording your dreams is a crucial step in the dream journaling process, as it allows you to capture the raw material of your subconscious mind and begin to make sense of it. The art of recording dreams is a delicate one, requiring a combination of skill, patience, and dedication. In this section, we will explore the techniques and strategies for recording your dreams, as well as the importance of creating a consistent and effective dream recording routine.

The Importance of Recording Dreams

Recording your dreams is essential for several reasons. First and foremost, it allows you to capture the fleeting nature of dreams, which can quickly fade from memory if not written down. By recording your dreams, you can preserve the details and emotions of the dream, even if they seem trivial or insignificant at first glance. Additionally, recording your dreams helps to develop your self-awareness and introspection skills, allowing you to tap into your subconscious mind and gain insight into your thoughts, feelings, and behaviors.

Techniques for Recording Dreams

There are several techniques for recording dreams, each with its own unique advantages and disadvantages. One of the most popular methods is the "stream-of-consciousness" approach, where you write down your dreams as soon as you wake up, without stopping to think or reflect. This approach helps to capture the raw, unfiltered nature of your dreams, but can be challenging to read and interpret later on. Another approach is the "structured" method, where you use a template or outline to record your dreams. This approach helps to organize your thoughts and ensure that you capture all the relevant details, but can feel too rigid or formulaic for some people.

Tips for Recording Dreams

Regardless of the technique you choose, there are several tips to keep in mind when recording your dreams. First and foremost, write down your dreams as soon as possible after waking up. The longer you wait, the more details you'll forget, and the less vivid your dreams will become. Second, be as descriptive as possible when recording your dreams. Use all your senses to bring the dream to life, and try to capture the emotions and sensations you experienced during the dream. Finally, don't worry too much about grammar, spelling, or syntax when recording your dreams. The goal is to capture the raw material of your subconscious mind, not to create a polished piece of writing.

Identifying Recurring Themes

Identifying recurring themes in your dreams is a crucial step in unlocking the secrets of your subconscious mind. By recognizing patterns and themes that appear repeatedly in your dreams, you can gain insight into your thoughts, feelings, and behaviors, and develop a deeper understanding of yourself and the world around you.

The Importance of Identifying Recurring Themes

Identifying recurring themes in your dreams is essential for several reasons. First and foremost, it allows you to tap into the subconscious mind's ability to process and consolidate information, revealing patterns and connections that may not be immediately apparent in your waking life. By recognizing recurring themes, you can gain insight into your motivations, desires, and fears, and develop a deeper understanding of your thoughts, feelings, and behaviors. Additionally, identifying recurring themes can help you identify areas of your life where you may be stuck or stagnant, and provide guidance on how to move forward. By recognizing patterns and themes that appear repeatedly in your dreams, you can develop a greater sense of self-awareness and introspection, allowing you to make positive changes in your life.

Techniques for Identifying Recurring Themes

There are several techniques for identifying recurring themes in your dreams. One of the most effective methods is to keep a dream journal, where you record your dreams and look for patterns and themes over time. You can also use a dream dictionary or symbolism guide to help you interpret the symbols and themes that appear in your dreams. Another technique is to practice mindfulness and meditation, which can help you develop a greater sense of self-awareness and introspection. By cultivating a greater understanding of your thoughts, feelings, and behaviors, you can gain insight into the recurring themes and patterns that appear in your dreams.

Tips for Identifying Recurring Themes

There are several tips to keep in mind when identifying recurring themes in your dreams. First and foremost, be patient and persistent. Identifying recurring themes takes time and practice, so don't get discouraged if you don't see immediate results. Additionally, be open-minded and non-judgmental. Recurring themes can reveal deep-seated fears, desires, and motivations, so be prepared to confront uncomfortable truths about yourself. Finally, use your intuition and trust your instincts. If you feel like a particular theme or pattern is significant, trust your instincts and explore it further.

PART 3: THE ETHICAL LANDSCAPE OF HYPER-MEMORY

The realm of dreams has long been a source of fascination and intrigue for humans. From the vivid, surreal landscapes of our subconscious mind to the mysterious, often inexplicable events that unfold within them, dreams have captivated our imagination and inspired our creativity. But beyond their role as a source of artistic inspiration or a window into our subconscious mind, dreams also hold a profound power to shape our lives and inform our understanding of ourselves and the world around us.

As we navigate the complexities of our waking lives, dreams offer a unique perspective on our thoughts, feelings, and experiences. They provide a safe space for us to process and consolidate information, to work through challenges and emotions, and to gain insight into our motivations and desires. But dreams are not just a passive reflection of our waking lives; they also hold the power to shape and influence our thoughts, feelings, and behaviors in profound ways.

The ability to consciously access and manipulate memories within dreams offers a powerful tool for personal growth, healing, and transformation. By tapping into the subconscious mind's ability to process and consolidate information, we can gain insight into our thoughts, feelings, and behaviors, and develop a deeper understanding of ourselves and the world around us. But this power also raises important ethical concerns, particularly around issues of privacy, trauma re-experiencing, and the potential for misuse.

In this section, we will explore the ethical implications of consciously accessing and manipulating deeply personal memories within dreams. We will consider the potential benefits and risks of this practice, and examine the issues of privacy, trauma re-experiencing, and misuse that arise when we tap into the subconscious mind's ability to process and consolidate information. By exploring these ethical concerns, we can develop a deeper understanding of the power and the peril of consciously accessing and manipulating memories within dreams, and cultivate a more responsible and ethical approach to this practice.

THE POWER OF MEMORY MANIPULATION

Memory manipulation within dreams has the potential to be a powerful tool for personal growth, healing, and transformation. By consciously accessing and manipulating memories within dreams, individuals can tap into the subconscious mind's ability to process and consolidate information, and gain insight into their thoughts, feelings, and behaviors.

Benefits of Memory Manipulation

There are several benefits to memory manipulation within dreams, including:

- Overcoming phobias and anxieties: By confronting and manipulating memories related to phobias and anxieties within dreams, individuals can begin to overcome these fears and develop greater confidence and self-assurance.

- Enhancing creativity and problem-solving skills: Memory manipulation within dreams can allow individuals to tap into the subconscious mind's creative potential, leading to new insights and innovative solutions to problems.

- Improving emotional regulation and well-being: By manipulating memories related to emotional experiences within dreams, individuals can gain greater insight into their emotional patterns and develop more effective strategies for managing their emotions.

- Resolving past traumas: Memory manipulation within dreams can provide a safe and controlled environment for individuals to confront and resolve past traumas, leading to greater healing and closure.

Techniques for Memory Manipulation There are several techniques for memory manipulation within dreams, including:

- Lucid dreaming: This involves becoming aware that you are dreaming and taking control of the dream narrative.

- Dream incubation: This involves focusing on a specific theme or issue before sleep and allowing the subconscious mind to process and consolidate information during the dream state.

- Wake-back-to-bed technique: This involves setting an alarm to wake up after a few hours of sleep, staying awake for a short period, and then going back to bed to induce a lucid dream state. By mastering these techniques and harnessing the power of memory manipulation within dreams, individuals can tap into the subconscious mind's vast potential for growth, healing, and transformation.

THE PERIL OF MEMORY MANIPULATION

While memory manipulation within dreams holds great potential for personal growth and healing, it also poses significant risks and ethical concerns. As we explore the potential benefits of this practice, it is essential to acknowledge the potential perils and take steps to mitigate them.

Privacy and Confidentiality Issues

One of the most significant concerns surrounding memory manipulation within dreams is the potential for privacy and confidentiality issues. When individuals access and manipulate memories within dreams, they may be exposing themselves to sensitive and personal information that could be exploited by others. This is particularly concerning in cases where individuals may be sharing their dreams with others, such as in a therapeutic setting or online community.

To mitigate this risk, it is essential to establish clear boundaries and guidelines for sharing dreams and personal information. Individuals should be cautious about sharing their dreams with others, and should only do so in a secure and confidential setting. Therapists and practitioners working with clients should also establish clear guidelines for confidentiality and informed consent.

Trauma Re-Experiencing and Emotional Distress

Another significant concern surrounding memory manipulation within dreams is the potential for trauma re-experiencing and emotional distress. When individuals access and manipulate memories within dreams, they may be exposing themselves to traumatic or distressing experiences that could trigger emotional distress. To mitigate this risk, it is essential to establish clear guidelines for working with traumatic memories within dreams. Individuals should only access and manipulate traumatic memories within dreams under the guidance of a qualified therapist or practitioner, and should take steps to establish a safe and supportive environment for processing and integrating traumatic experiences.

Potential for Misuse and Manipulation by Others

Finally, there is also a risk that memory manipulation within dreams could be misused or manipulated by others. This could include using dream manipulation techniques to extract sensitive information from individuals, or to influence their thoughts and behaviors. To mitigate this risk, it is essential to establish clear guidelines for the use of dream manipulation techniques, and to ensure that individuals are fully informed and consenting before engaging in any dream manipulation activities. It is also essential to establish clear boundaries and guidelines for sharing dreams and personal information, and to ensure that dream manipulation techniques are only used in a safe and supportive environment.

THE COLLECTIVE UNCONSCIOUS

The concept of the collective unconscious has long fascinated philosophers, psychologists, and scientists alike. First proposed by Carl Jung, the collective unconscious refers to a shared reservoir of archetypes and experiences that are common to all humans, regardless of their cultural, linguistic, or geographical backgrounds. According to Jung, the collective unconscious is a universal, collective memory that contains the experiences of our ancestors, as well as the archetypes that are present in the dreams and myths of all cultures.

The idea of a collective unconscious has far-reaching implications for our understanding of human consciousness and the nature of reality. If we accept that there is a shared reservoir of archetypes and experiences that are common to all humans, then we must also consider the possibility that our individual experiences are not entirely our own. Instead, they may be influenced by a collective, universal consciousness that shapes our perceptions, thoughts, and emotions.

The concept of shared dream experiences is particularly relevant to the idea of a collective unconscious. If we can share dreams with others, then it suggests that our individual experiences are not entirely our own, but are instead connected to a larger, collective consciousness. This raises fascinating questions about the nature of reality and the interconnectedness of all things.

In this section, we will explore the concept of shared dream experiences and their potential implications for our understanding of the collective unconscious. We will examine the evidence for shared dream experiences, and consider the various explanations for this phenomenon. We will also speculate on the broader implications of shared dream experiences, and consider the potential insights they may offer into the nature of reality and the collective unconscious.

The concept of the collective unconscious was first introduced by Carl Jung, a Swiss psychiatrist and psychoanalyst, in the early 20th century. According to Jung, the collective unconscious is a shared reservoir of archetypes and experiences that are common to all humans, regardless of their cultural, linguistic, or geographical backgrounds. These archetypes are thought to be universal, collective memories that are present in the unconscious mind of every individual, and are believed to be the source of many of the symbols, themes, and motifs that appear in dreams, myths, and legends.

Jung believed that archetypes are the building blocks of the collective unconscious, and that they are present in the unconscious mind of every individual. Archetypes are thought to be universal, collective memories that are present in the unconscious mind of every individual, and are believed to be the source of many of the symbols, themes, and motifs that appear in dreams, myths, and legends. Examples of archetypes include the Mother, the Father, the Child, the Trickster, and the Hero.

Jung believed that the collective unconscious is a shared reservoir of archetypes and experiences that are common to all humans. This reservoir is thought to be present in the unconscious mind of every individual, and is believed to be the source of many of the symbols, themes, and motifs that appear in dreams, myths, and legends. The collective unconscious is thought to be a universal, collective memory that contains the experiences of our ancestors, as well as the archetypes that are present in the dreams and myths of all cultures.

The concept of the collective unconscious has far-reaching implications for our understanding of human consciousness and the nature of reality. If we accept that there is a shared reservoir of archetypes and experiences that are common to all humans, then we must also consider the possibility that our individual experiences are not entirely our own. Instead, they may be influenced by a collective, universal consciousness that shapes our perceptions, thoughts, and emotions. This raises fascinating questions about the nature of reality and the interconnectedness of all things.

Printed in Dunstable, United Kingdom